MICHIGAN TRIVIA

MICHIGAN TRIVIA

COMPILED BY
ERNIE & JILL COUCH

Copyright © 1989 by Ernie Couch

Published in Nashville, Tennessee, by Rutledge Hill Press, 513 Third Avenue South, Nashville, Tennessee 37210

Typography by Bailey Typography, Inc.
Cover photography by Doug Brachey Photography
Color Separation by Manning Camera Graphics
Book and cover design by Ernie Couch/Consultx

Library of Congress Cataloging-in-Publication Data

Couch, Ernie, 1949–
  Michigan trivia / compiled by Ernie & Jill Couch.
    p. cm.
  ISBN 0-934395-97-7
    1. Michigan—Miscellanea. 2. Questions and answers.
  I. Couch, Jill, 1948–   . II. Title.
F566.5.C68 1988
977.4—dc19   88-36901
                                    CIP

Printed in the United States of America
1 2 3 4 5 6 7 8 — 94 93 92 91 90 89

PREFACE

Michigan, former part of the Northwest Territory, is far more than just the automobile manufacturing capital of the nation. The state's colorful and compelling history speaks of a richly diversified land and people. Captured within these pages are some of the highlights of this rich heritage, both the well-known and the not-so-well-known.

Michigan Trivia is designed to be informative, educational, and entertaining. Most of all, we hope reading this book will motivate you to learn more about the great state of Michigan.

Ernie and Jill Couch

To
Phil & Susan Knebel
and
the great people of Michigan

TABLE OF CONTENTS

GEOGRAPHY

Q. In what Michigan county did the last stagecoach holdup in the United States take place on August 16, 1889?

A. Gogebic.

———◆———

Q. The copper mining community Ahmeek took its name from an Indian word having what meaning?

A. "Beaver."

———◆———

Q. What Michigan city is the only municipality in the state to have been under the flags of France, England, Spain, and the United States?

A. Niles.

———◆———

Q. The Porcupine Mountains are often called by what nickname?

A. "The Porkies."

———◆———

Q. Automotive industry innovator Preston Thomas Tucker was born in what Michigan community on September 21, 1903?

A. Capac.

Q. The Mackinac Bridge is how many miles in length?

A. Five.

Q. What irregular land mass lies between Lake Michigan and Big Bay de Noc?

A. The Garden Peninsula.

Q. How many islands make up the Les Cheneaux group?

A. Thirty-five.

Q. Quaker settlers named what present-day Detroit suburb for their hometown in New York in 1824?

A. Farmington.

Q. "Hill near the creek," is the meaning of which Houghton County Indian place name?

A. Sidnaw.

Q. What two new names for Lansing did the Michigan legislature recommend in 1847?

A. Michigan and Michigamme.

Q. What city founded by fur trader Louis Chappée in 1796 is the southernmost town in the Upper Peninsula?

A. Menominee.

Q. What Michigan community grew from 3,589 to 45,615 residents from 1910 to 1920, leading the nation in growth during that period?

A. Hamtramck.

———◆———

Q. What Gogebic County community is situated at the apex of three major watersheds?

A. Watersmeet.

———◆———

Q. Marquette was first known by what name?

A. Worcester.

———◆———

Q. What Cheboygan County community is named in honor of a Potawatomi Indian chief who provided land for the building of Fort Dearborn, now Chicago, Illinois?

A. Topinabee.

———◆———

Q. During the lumber boom era, what name was given to the row of saloons that lined Water Street in Bay City?

A. "Hell's Half Mile."

———◆———

Q. What Delta County community was founded in 1880 by fishermen from Saint Martin Island?

A. Fairport.

———◆———

Q. On Christmas Eve, 1913, in what community were seventy-two women and children trampled to death when a false fire alarm was sounded during a strike meeting?

A. Calumet.

Q. What is the southwesternmost county in the state?

A. Berrien.

Q. What Michigan city contains the only model pet cemetery in the world?

A. Gladstone.

Q. The Saginaw Bay community of Quanicassee took its name from an Indian word having what meaning?

A. "Lone tree."

Q. The religious sect, Israelite House of David, used what island in the Beaver Archipelago as a penal colony for dissenters?

A. High.

Q. What was the former name of Kingston?

A. Newburg.

Q. In what Michigan city did Thomas A. Edison learn telegraphy?

A. Mount Clemens.

Q. The sound made by water pouring over rocks in a local stream gave rise to the name of what Saint Clair County community?

A. Rattle Run.

Q. In 1936 what Upper Peninsula city processed 100,000 square feet of bird's-eye maple for use in the English steamship, S.S. *Queen Mary?*

A. Escanaba.

Q. What northern Huron County community became famous during the 1800s for the high quality abrasive stones it produced?

A. Grindstone City.

Q. Bronson was the first seat of what county?

A. Branch.

Q. What is the largest U.S.-owned island within the Saint Clair Flats?

A. Harsens Island.

Q. Lapeer and Lapeer County derive their names from a corruption of what two French words?

A. La Pierre ("the stone").

Q. What Otsego County community founded in 1870 was named for a prominent eastern family?

A. Vanderbilt.

Q. Monroe, which was named in honor of President James Monroe, was formerly known by what name?

A. Frenchtown.

Q. When the Territory of Michigan was created on January 11, 1805, what town was selected as its capital?

A. Detroit.

———◆———

Q. What Luce County community is named for a one-time lumber camp cook who became a shipping magnate?

A. Dollarville (for Robert Dollar).

———◆———

Q. Isle Royale is in which of the Great Lakes?

A. Lake Superior.

———◆———

Q. What Tuscola County community is named in honor of the founder of a well-known New York university?

A. Vassar (for Matthew Vassar).

———◆———

Q. What community established in 1852 is the oldest incorporated settlement on the Keweenaw Peninsula?

A. Houghton.

———◆———

Q. What was the first settlement in Lenawee County?

A. Tecumseh.

———◆———

Q. The community of Nahma on Big Bay de Noc is named for an Indian word of what meaning?

A. "Sturgeon."

Q. What north Eaton County town received its name from a large sandstone formation on the Grand River?

A. Grand Ledge.

Q. Where was the childhood home of reformer and suffragist Anna Howard Shaw?

A. Ashton.

Q. What is the largest island in the Detroit River?

A. Grosse Ile.

Q. The Upper Michigan community of Greenland was originally given what name?

A. Maplewood.

Q. What Lake Michigan community gained fame for feeding stranded motorists pancakes for several days during a December, 1937, blizzard?

A. Glenn.

Q. Jackson is a shortened version of what early name?

A. Jacksonopolis.

Q. Where in 1846 was the first ferry landing established on Portage Lake?

A. Ripley.

Q. In the late 1800s the much-touted therapeutic quality of the local mineral water led to the development of a booming spa and health resort industry for what Gratiot County community?

A. Saint Louis.

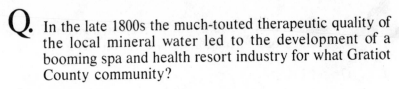

Q. What southern Ionia County community received its name from a city in Russia?

A. Lake Odessa.

Q. Christmas is in what Upper Peninsula county?

A. Alger.

Q. Where was the first Michigan parish for German-speaking Roman Catholics founded in 1836?

A. Westphalia.

Q. What southwestern community is known as the "Gateway to Michigan"?

A. New Buffalo.

Q. By what previous name was Stephenson known?

A. Little River.

Q. Arthur Hendrick, who became president pro-tem of the U.S. Senate in 1947, was born in what Michigan city?

A. Grand Rapids.

Q. What Ottawa County community changed its name from Berlin during World War I?

A. Marne.

Q. What Oakland County community received its name from a large manufacturing city in England?

A. Birmingham.

Q. Bloomfield Hills was first known by what name?

A. Bagley's Corners.

Q. Tahquamenon Falls is nearest to what Michigan community?

A. Paradise.

Q. The town of Clare and Clare County derive their names from a county in what country?

A. Ireland.

Q. What Michigan community earned its name by being a sheep slaughtering and processing center for the Detroit market?

A. Muttonville.

Q. During the late 1800s what planned city failed to develop between Grand Haven and Holland on Pigeon Lake?

A. Port Sheldon.

Q. President Gerald R. Ford grew up and later practiced law in what Michigan city?

A. Grand Rapids.

———◆———

Q. Lakes Huron and Superior are connected by what river?

A. Saint Marys.

———◆———

Q. Michigan is made up of how many counties?

A. Eighty-three.

———◆———

Q. The only authentic operating Dutch windmill in the nation is found in what Michigan city?

A. Holland (Windmill Island Municipal Park).

———◆———

Q. Where was actor Danny Thomas born?

A. Deerfield.

———◆———

Q. What is the largest stream on Beaver Island?

A. River Jordan.

———◆———

Q. How many international airports does Michigan have?

A. Four.

Q. In its resort heyday, what city on the Clinton River was known as "Michigan's spa"?

A. Mount Clemens.

———◆———

Q. At the mouth of what river on Hammond Bay did the Chippewa Indians hold ceremonies for the voluntary disposition of crippled and aged tribe members?

A. Ocqueoc.

———◆———

Q. What was the first mining community on the Marquette Range?

A. Negaunee.

———◆———

Q. In 1832 Congress authorized the removal of the Detroit arsenal to what nearby community?

A. Dearborn.

———◆———

Q. What large island is situated at the tip of the Upper Peninsula?

A. Drummond.

———◆———

Q. Where is the world's only marble lighthouse?

A. Belle Isle (Livingstone Lighthouse).

———◆———

Q. To oblige the railroad, Brimley was first given what name?

A. Superior.

Q. What nickname has been given to the Mackinac Bridge?

A. "Mighty Mac."

Q. Bronson Harbor, haughtily called "Bungtown Harbor" because barrel bungs were manufactured there, later became what city?

A. Benton Harbor.

Q. What village combined with East Jordan in 1887?

A. South Arm.

Q. The Michigan Iron Industry Museum is in what Upper Peninsula community?

A. Negaunee.

Q. What community was the first seat of Hillsdale County?

A. Jonesville.

Q. Utica was originally known by what name?

A. Hog's Hollow.

Q. Indians spear-fishing by torch light led to the naming of what Antrim County lake?

A. Torch.

Q. What Michigan city has been called the "Cereal Bowl of America"?

A. Battle Creek.

Q. How many counties make up the southern border of Michigan?

A. Seven.

Q. The largest cement plant in the nation is in what Michigan city?

A. Alpena.

Q. Henry Chamberlain founded what Berrien County town?

A. Three Oaks.

Q. The nation's largest plant for producing bowling alley equipment is located in what Michigan city?

A. Muskegon.

Q. What is the greatest north–south distance in the Lower Peninsula?

A. 286 miles.

Q. What Alger County community was named for the local postmistress?

A. Sundell (for Sally Sundell Harsila).

Q. Due to Charles Kimberly's culture, refinement, and objection to the usage of obscene language, what Saginaw County community was named in his honor?

A. Saint Charles.

———◆———

Q. Sandusky is the seat of what Michigan county?

A. Sanilac.

———◆———

Q. What Keweenaw Peninsula community was named for a naval vessel?

A. Kearsarge (for the U.S.S. *Kearsarge*).

———◆———

Q. Rick, in Delta County, previously was known by what name?

A. Maple Ridge.

———◆———

Q. What Michigan community lost 76 business buildings and 243 homes during a two-hour fire in 1871?

A. Holland.

———◆———

Q. What Houghton County community is named after a French word referring to an Indian peace pipe?

A. Calumet.

———◆———

Q. By what name was Edenville known during lumbering days?

A. Camp Sixteen.

Q. What Lake Superior community bears an Indian name meaning "place of the big island"?

A. Munising.

———◆———

Q. Where in 1844 did the Free Will Baptists establish Michigan Central College, Michigan's first coeducational college?

A. Spring Arbor.

———◆———

Q. Michigan has how many international seaports?

A. Five (Port Huron, Bay City–Saginaw, Muskegon, Sault Sainte Marie, and Detroit).

———◆———

Q. Mail-order and department store magnate Montgomery Ward was a native of what Michigan city?

A. Niles.

———◆———

Q. For whom are the city of Wayne and Wayne County named?

A. General "Mad Anthony" Wayne.

———◆———

Q. Where is the largest Coast Guard station on the Great Lakes?

A. Sault Sainte Marie.

———◆———

Q. In 1839 what town was designated by the Michigan state senate as the state capital, only to have the measure defeated in the house?

A. Marshall.

Q. In January of 1847 fifty-three Dutch immigrants under the leadership of Dr. A. C. Van Raalte founded what settlement in Michigan?

A. Holland.

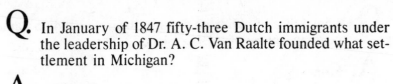

Q. Gros Cap, near Saint Ignace, took its name from a French name having what meaning?

A. "Big cape."

Q. What Michigan city is situated on the northwest shore of Thunder Bay?

A. Alpena.

Q. The Ojibway Indian burial ground is near what Upper Peninsula community?

A. Gaastra.

Q. Lansing was named in honor of a community in what state?

A. New York (from Chancellor John Lansing).

Q. Onaway took its name from an Indian word of what meaning?

A. "Awake."

Q. The Rix Robinson trading post evolved into what present-day community?

A. Ada.

Q. Where in the Keweenaw Peninsula was a company established in 1862 for the manufacture of a "secret formula" blasting fuse?

A. Eagle River.

Q. What is the highest range of mountains in Michigan?

A. The Porcupine Mountains.

Q. Grand Valley State College is in what Michigan community?

A. Allendale.

Q. What was the original seat of Alger County?

A. Au Train.

Q. What nickname was given Brevort, which served as a steamship freight storage site during the 1880s?

A. "The warehouse."

Q. What is the largest city in the Upper Peninsula?

A. Marquette.

Q. At the mouth of what river did Sieur de La Salle erect Fort Miami (or Miamis) in 1679?

A. Saint Joseph (Miami).

Q. During the "roaring eighties" lumber boom, what Michigan city was labeled with such titles as "Lumber Queen," "Red Light Queen," "Saloon Queen," and "Gambling Queen"?

A. Muskegon.

Q. In 1844 the first settlers gave what name to present-day Port Sanilac?

A. Bark Shanty Point.

Q. What Ottawa County community is named for a province of the Netherlands?

A. Zeeland.

Q. The home offices of Life Savers candy, Beech-Nut gum, and Squirt soft drink are in what Michigan city?

A. Holland.

Q. What Little Traverse Bay community was originated as a retreat and assembly facility of the Methodist Church in 1876?

A. Bay View.

Q. The Michigan School for the Deaf is in what city?

A. Flint.

Q. What was the name of the co-operative community established at Comstock by followers of François Fourier in 1844?

A. Arkadelphia Association.

Q. What lake did the Mormons use for baptisimal rites during their occupation of Beaver Island?

A. Font.

---◆---

Q. In 1690 Father Claude Aveneau explored the upper reaches of the Saint Joseph River and established a mission at the present-day site of what town?

A. Niles.

---◆---

Q. In what Michigan county is the Point Iroquois Light Station situated?

A. Chippewa.

---◆---

Q. The place name *Kawkawlin* in Bay County is the Indian word for what type of fish?

A. Pickerel.

---◆---

Q. What is the meaning of the German place name of Frankenmuth?

A. "Courage of the Franconians."

---◆---

Q. Homestead is at the southern tip of what island?

A. Sugar.

---◆---

Q. What international bridge crosses the Saint Clair River at Port Huron?

A. Blue Water Bridge.

Q. When Battle Creek was incorporated as a city in 1859, what new name was rejected by the electorate?

A. Waupakisco.

Q. Where in Dickinson County were the richest deposits of Menominee hematite discovered in 1878?

A. Iron Mountain.

Q. In 1856 what Potawatomi Indian mission was established near Hartford?

A. Saint Dominic's.

Q. What Houghton County community was obviously named for three local peaks?

A. Trimountain.

Q. *Menominee* is an Indian word of what meaning?

A. "Wild rice country."

Q. What coastline has been given the name "Graveyard of the Great Lakes"?

A. Whitefish Point on Lake Superior.

Q. Under the Northwest Territorial Government what county embraced all of the Michigan region?

A. Wayne.

Q. At 1,980 feet above sea level, what is the highest elevation in Michigan?

A. Mount Curwood (Baraga County).

Q. Singer Betty Hutton was born February 26, 1921, in what Michigan city?

A. Battle Creek.

Q. Michigan's paper manufacturing industry is centered in what city?

A. Kalamazoo.

Q. Bronson was the name of what Michigan city between 1829 and 1836?

A. Kalamazoo.

Q. Whitefish Point is a portion of what county?

A. Chippewa.

Q. North Manitou Island and South Manitou Island share an Indian name having what meaning?

A. "Spirit."

Q. Where is Suomi College, the only Finnish college in the United States, located?

A. Hancock (Houghton County).

Q. Such settlements as Beebe's Corners, Ridgeway, and Lenox have evolved into what present-day Michigan community?

A. Richmond.

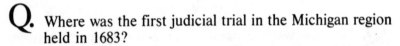

Q. What is the meaning of the French place name *Detroit?*

A. "The strait."

Q. What community served as the seat of Clare County prior to Harrison?

A. Farwell.

Q. Where was the first judicial trial in the Michigan region held in 1683?

A. Saint Ignace.

Q. What Crawford County community is named for a popular Michigan game fish of the 1800s?

A. Grayling.

Q. Where did Michigan's first major sitdown strike take place on December 30, 1936?

A. Fisher Body Plant No. 1 (in Flint).

Q. What fortification was established by Antoine de la Mothe Cadillac at the "place du detroit" on July 24, 1701?

A. Fort Pontchartrain.

Q. The construction of a large shingle mill in 1887 brought what new name to the community of Jeroneville?

A. Shingleton.

Q. What community in Baraga County is named for a province of Sweden?

A. Skanee.

Q. During the copper boom, what was the chief port of entry into the "copper country" of the Keweenaw Peninsula?

A. Copper Harbor.

Q. What bridge connects Michigan with Canada at Detroit?

A. The Ambassador Bridge.

Q. Near the present-day site of what Michigan town did Father Jacques Marquette die on May 18, 1675, at the age of thirty-eight?

A. Ludington.

Q. What is the largest arm of Lake Michigan?

A. Green Bay.

Q. Wild Fowl Bay is on the west coast of what county?

A. Huron.

Q. What is the meaning of the Indian words *michi-guma* from which Michigan is derived?

A. "Big water" or "great lake."

———◆———

Q. Where did Darius Clark construct the first sawmill in Delta County in 1847?

A. Masonville.

———◆———

Q. What city in Gogebic County was platted by the Milwaukee, Lake Shore & Western Railway Company in 1885?

A. Ironwood.

———◆———

Q. Where did the first congregation of Baptists in Michigan establish themselves in 1822?

A. Pontiac.

———◆———

Q. Antrim was originally called by what name?

A. Furnaceville.

———◆———

Q. The corruption of a local trapper's name led to the name of what Mecosta County community?

A. Paris (from John Parish).

———◆———

Q. Big Rapids, seat of Mecosta County, was first called by what name?

A. Leonard.

Q. What country was the first to receive an exported United States automobile in 1893?

A. India (a steam car built by Ranson E. Olds).

----◆----

Q. How many counties does the Upper Peninsula have?

A. Fifteen.

----◆----

Q. Where is Ferris State College situated?

A. Big Rapids.

----◆----

Q. By what name was Grand Rapids called for a short time in the early 1840s?

A. Kent.

----◆----

Q. The finding of a broken ax by a survey party led to the naming of what Michigan community?

A. Bad Axe.

----◆----

Q. To settle the "Toledo War" in 1837, what land concession was given Michigan by the U.S. government to compensate for the loss of the "Toledo strip" to Ohio?

A. The Upper Peninsula.

----◆----

Q. Every Simplicity sewing pattern in the world is produced in what Michigan city?

A. Niles.

Q. Richard Ford was the first known settler of what Detroit suburb?

A. Highland Park.

———◆———

Q. In what county in 1860 was the first successful well drilled in Michigan for the extraction of salt brine?

A. Saginaw.

———◆———

Q. Lake Erie is named for an Indian word having what meaning?

A. "Cat."

———◆———

Q. Through what narrows does Lake Michigan empty into Lake Huron?

A. The Straits of Mackinac.

———◆———

Q. Where was the first military outpost established in Michigan around 1671?

A. Saint Ignace.

———◆———

Q. By the 1890s, what Michigan city was producing one hundred thousand carriages and related vehicles a year?

A. Flint.

———◆———

Q. Petoskey is an English approximation of what Indian name?

A. Bidasiga ("rising sun").

Q. A replica of the 1893 World's Fair "Load of Logs" is displayed in what Ontonagon County community?

A. Ewen.

———◆———

Q. Until 1907, Scottville was concurrently known by what two additional names?

A. Mason Center and Sweetland.

———◆———

Q. The River Raisin flows through what Michigan city?

A. Monroe.

———◆———

Q. What is the seat of Lake County?

A. Baldwin.

———◆———

Q. Where was the first permanent settlement founded by Europeans in Michigan in 1668?

A. Sault Sainte Marie.

———◆———

Q. In what Ionia County town was author Clarence Budington Kelland born on July 11, 1881?

A. Portland.

———◆———

Q. What Osceola County community was settled primarily by immigrants fleeing the German revolution of 1848?

A. Reed City.

Q. What Saint Clair County community was named for the traditional founder of the Inca Empire?

A. Capac (for Mamco Capac).

Q. Manistique is the seat of what Upper Peninsula county?

A. Schoolcraft.

Q. Where did the first German family settle in the Michigan region in 1751?

A. Grosse Pointe.

Q. The name of what Michigan community appears on early maps in such forms as Sikonam, Sakonam, Saguinam, and Saquinam?

A. Saginaw.

Q. Near what present-day city was the last great Indian battle in central Michigan fought in 1830 between the Chippewa and Sauk?

A. Midland.

Q. "Place of entrance, portage of harbor," is the meaning of what county and community name?

A. Cheboygan.

Q. In 1907 what community was established in Marquette County by the Cleveland Cliffs Iron Company?

A. Gwinn.

Q. During the prohibition era what Michigan community became the number one point of entry for illicit Canadian liquors into the United States?

A. Ecorse.

Q. What Alpena County community derives its name from the corruption of an Indian word meaning "image stones"?

A. Ossineke (from *wawsinkee*).

Q. Named for a local mid-1860s academy, Disco is in what county?

A. Macomb.

Q. Moran, in Mackinac County, was first called by what name?

A. Jacobs City.

Q. What is the meaning of the Indian place name Quinnesec situated near the Wisconsin border?

A. "Smoking river."

Q. Pine Stump Junction is in what county?

A. Luce.

Q. Originally called Lamb's Corners, what Lapeer County community was renamed in honor of an English poet?

A. Dryden (for John Dryden).

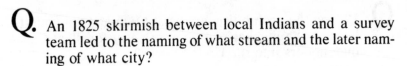

Q. An 1825 skirmish between local Indians and a survey team led to the naming of what stream and the later naming of what city?

A. Battle Creek.

———◆———

Q. What lagoon is at the upper east end of Belle Isle?

A. Blue Heron.

———◆———

Q. What Washtenaw County city was named in honor of a nineteenth-century Greek military hero?

A. Ypsilanti (for General Demetrios Ypsilanti).

———◆———

Q. On what river is Bay City situated?

A. Saginaw.

———◆———

Q. In what southern Michigan city were such automobiles as the Briscoe, Cutting, Clark–Carter, Imperial, Jackson, and Earl once manufactured?

A. Jackson.

———◆———

Q. Averill was known by what previous name derived from a local saloon?

A. Red Keg.

———◆———

Q. What Dickinson County community is named for the Roman god of metal workers?

A. Vulcan.

Q. What southeastern Huron County "phantom city" was greatly advertised by land promoters in the Detroit area during 1835 and 1836?

A. White Rock.

———◆———

Q. Luce and Mackinac counties share what large lake?

A. Manistique.

———◆———

Q. By what name was the early fishing settlement that later evolved into Charlevoix known?

A. Pine River.

———◆———

Q. Two early settlers talking about the natural beauty of the area led to the naming of what Chippewa County community?

A. Paradise.

———◆———

Q. What Mackinac County community has an Indian name meaning "the mocker" or "place of echoes"?

A. Naubinway.

———◆———

Q. By what other name has the Schoolcraft County community of Gulliver been known?

A. Whitedale.

———◆———

Q. What Menominee County community is named in honor of a civil engineer of the Chicago & Northwestern Railroad of the 1870s?

A. Powers (for Edward Powers).

Q. What is the Michigan state motto?

A. *Si quaeris peninsulam amoenam, circumspice* (If you seek a pleasant peninsula, look about you).

———◆———

Q. Singing legend Stevie Wonder was born in what Michigan city?

A. Saginaw.

———◆———

Q. What is Michigan's largest port?

A. Detroit.

———◆———

Q. Under what name was Onaway originally founded in 1881?

A. Shaw Post Office.

———◆———

Q. What bridge connects the Upper and Lower peninsulas of Michigan?

A. Mackinac Bridge.

———◆———

Q. Television personality Bob Eubanks was born in what Michigan city?

A. Flint.

———◆———

Q. What Michigan city is known nationally for its production of baby food?

A. Fremont.

Q. Battle Creek evolved from what 1831 settlement?

A. Milton.

———————◆———————

Q. What Huron County community was known during the era of wildcat money for its production of large quantities of counterfeit United States and Mexican currency?

A. Harbor Beach.

———————◆———————

Q. A derivative from the Indian word for "little rock" is the name of what Baraga County community?

A. Assinins.

———————◆———————

Q. Where was General William Rufus Shafter, head of the Santiago campaign during the Spanish–American War, born?

A. Galesburg.

———————◆———————

Q. What name is given to the Pinconning River on many old maps?

A. Potato River.

———————◆———————

Q. Parma, established in 1838, was known by what early name?

A. Cracker Hill.

———————◆———————

Q. From what Potawatomi Indian leader did the community of Nottawa derive its name?

A. Chief Nottawaseepe.

Q. Michigan became part of what territory in 1800?

A. Indiana Territory.

———◆———

Q. What Chippewa County community was settled at the junction of the Duluth, South Shore & Atlantic Railway and the Minneapolis, Saint Paul & Sault Sainte Marie Railway in 1881?

A. Trout Lake.

———◆———

Q. How many of the Great Lakes border the state of Michigan?

A. Four (Erie, Huron, Michigan, and Superior)

———◆———

Q. What city serves as the capital for the state of Michigan?

A. Lansing.

———◆———

Q. Ontonagon is an Indian place name having what meaning?

A. "Place of the bowl."

———◆———

Q. What was the first settlement in Benzie County?

A. Benzonia.

———◆———

Q. Prior to developing into a village, what Hillsdale County community was designated by stagecoach travelers as the "Old Chicago Turnpike at the Kalamazoo River"?

A. Moscow.

Q. What Michigan community's name is derived from the initials of its eight founders.

A. Germfask.

Q. What community and body of water are named in honor of the original surveyor of Cheboygan County?

A. Mullett Lake.

Q. Six Lakes is in what county?

A. Montclam.

Q. The first Ford automobile dealer in the Upper Peninsula is honored in the name of what Michigan community?

A. Kingsford (for Edward G. Kingsford).

Q. What river connects Lake Erie and Lake Saint Clair?

A. Detroit River.

Q. Wooden Shoe Village is in what county?

A. Gladwin.

Q. "The high ground" is the meaning of what Indian place name?

A. Ishpeming.

Q. What is the greatest distance east to west in the Upper Peninsula?

A. 334 miles.

———◆———

Q. The world's largest limestone quarry is in what Michigan community?

A. Rogers City.

———◆———

Q. What Chippewa County community is named for a town in Ireland?

A. Dafter.

———◆———

Q. What is the most common nickname given to Michigan?

A. "The Wolverine State."

———◆———

Q. The Motown Sound had its beginnings in a converted home on what Detroit boulevard?

A. West Grand.

———◆———

Q. Where was television news personality Charles Collingwood born?

A. Three Rivers.

———◆———

Q. Michigan's own community of Bunker Hill is in what county?

A. Ingham.

ENTERTAINMENT

C H A P T E R T W O

Q. What Detroit native portrayed singer Billie Holiday in the 1973 film *Lady Sings the Blues?*

A. Diana Ross.

———◆———

Q. Amos Jacobs was the original name of what Deerfield-born television star?

A. Danny Thomas.

———◆———

Q. What role did Michigan-born actor Ray Teal play in the television series, "Bonanza"?

A. Sheriff Roy Coffee.

———◆———

Q. Debuting in 1936 over WWJ in Detroit, what crime fighting adventure series used "Flight of the Bumblebee" as its theme song?

A. "The Green Hornet."

———◆———

Q. What 1960s singer/composer was born Charles Westover in Grand Rapids on December 30, 1939?

A. Del Shannon.

Q. In the early 1970s, what Detroit-born drummer was involved in the "New Communications in Jazz," project that brought music to hundreds of thousands of high-school students across the nation?

A. Oliver Jackson.

◆

Q. "Lonely Teardrops" scored in the top ten for what Detroit native in 1959?

A. Jackie Wilson.

◆

Q. What Detroit-born actor appeared as Lance Prentiss in the TV soap opera "The Young and the Restless"?

A. Dennis Cole.

◆

Q. What 1973 album placed Detroit-born Donald Byrd into the mainstream of the pop–soul market?

A. *Black Byrd.*

◆

Q. The Supremes were originally known by what name?

A. The Primettes.

◆

Q. Originating over radio station WWJ in the early 1930s, what was the theme song of "The Lone Ranger"?

A. "William Tell Overture."

◆

Q. In 1974 what Detroit-born actress portrayed a poor but energetic waitress in *Alice Doesn't Live Here Anymore?*

A. Ellen Burstyn.

Q. What Detroit-born actress co-starred with Jane Fonda and Dolly Parton in the comedy film *Nine to Five?*

A. Lily Tomlin.

———◆———

Q. What Detroit-based male singing group was originally known as the Elgins?

A. The Temptations.

———◆———

Q. Where was character actor Ray Teal born?

A. Grand Rapids.

———◆———

Q. Michigan-born musician Rudy Rutherford was featured on clarinet with Count Basie in what mid–1940s movie?

A. *High Tide.*

———◆———

Q. What was Alice Cooper's first chart single?

A. "I'm Eighteen."

———◆———

Q. Top entertainers combine with local talent during what summer celebration at Chesaning?

A. Showboat Festival Week.

———◆———

Q. In what Michigan city was Stevie Wonder born on May 3, 1950?

A. Saginaw.

Q. Audrey Hepburn starred with what Detroit-born actor in the 1961 film *Breakfast at Tiffany's?*

A. George Peppard.

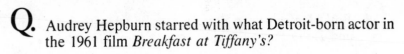

Q. What trio became Motown's most phenomenal song-writing–production team in the mid-to-late 1960s?

A. Eddie Holland, Lamont Dozier, and Brian Holland.

Q. What Detroit-born actor starred as Tod Stiles in the early 1960s adventure series *Route 66?*

A. Martin Milner.

Q. Where was jazz singer Earl Coleman born?

A. Port Huron.

Q. In 1988 what Detroit-born performer became mayor of Palm Springs, California?

A. Sonny Bono.

Q. What girls' group furnished most of the background vocals on Motown hits?

A. Andantes.

Q. Detroit-born actress Kim Hunter won an Academy Award for Best Supporting Actress in what 1951 film?

A. *A Streetcar Named Desire.*

Q. What 1987 six-hour miniseries was partially filmed in the Petoskey area and the Upper Peninsula?

A. "Hemingway."

Q. Detroit jazz educator Ernie Rodgers became known for his expertise on what instrument?

A. Saxophone.

Q. What vocalist officially replaced Florence Ballard as a Supreme in 1967?

A. Cindy Birdsong.

Q. What suspense thriller was the first feature motion picture to be made solely in western Michigan?

A. *Blind Faith*.

Q. What Michigan-formed band went to number one on the charts with the 1973 hit single "We're an American Band"?

A. Grand Funk.

Q. Blythe Danner starred with what Detroit-born actor in the 1982 film *Too Far to Go?*

A. Michael Moriarty.

Q. Who was considered Motown's first major female recording star?

A. Mary Wells.

Q. What character did Detroit-born actor Harry Morgan play on the long-running television series "M*A*S*H"?

A. Colonel Sherman Potter.

———◆———

Q. Detroit native Suzi Quatro portrayed what character on TV's "Happy Days"?

A. Leather Tuscadero.

———◆———

Q. What Michigan-born actress played Nellie Taft in the 1979 television miniseries "Backstairs at the White House"?

A. Julie Harris.

———◆———

Q. What hit by Madonna topped the charts in 1984?

A. "Like a Virgin."

———◆———

Q. What famous soul singer grew up singing in the choir of her father's New Bethel Church in Detroit?

A. Aretha Franklin.

———◆———

Q. "Shake, Rattle and Roll" and "Rock around the Clock" were hit singles by what Detroit-born musician?

A. Bill Haley.

———◆———

Q. Michigan-born Bob Eubanks became best known for hosting what successful game show?

A. "The Newlywed Game."

Q. Motown recording artists, the Jackson Five, debuted what record for the company in 1969?

A. "I Want You Back."

━━━━◆━━━━

Q. What Detroit native gained great popularity by singing in the Big Bands of Gene Krupa and Glenn Miller?

A. Johnny Desmond.

━━━━◆━━━━

Q. An Academy Award nomination went to what Detroit native for best supporting actress in the 1976 suspense film *Carrie?*

A. Piper Laurie.

━━━━◆━━━━

Q. What Detroit vocal group had a 1964 hit with their first Motown recording, "Baby I Need Your Loving"?

A. The Four Tops.

━━━━◆━━━━

Q. Gene Goldkette, legendary leader from the Big Band era, was owner of what one-time top Detroit night spot?

A. Greystone Ballroom.

━━━━◆━━━━

Q. In 1965 the recording of what song written, arranged, and produced by Sonny Bono became a number one hit on both sides of the Atlantic?

A. "I Got You Babe."

━━━━◆━━━━

Q. What Detroit-born musician considers "Journey in Satchidananda" and "Blue Nile" her two best works?

A. Alice Coltrane.

Q. What record became the first major success for the Temptations?

A. "The Way You Do the Things You Do."

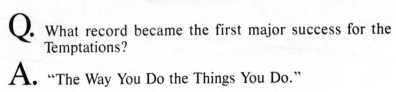

Q. Dancer-singer-actress Donna McKechnie received a Tony Award in 1976 for what Broadway play?

A. *A Chorus Line*.

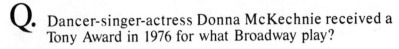

Q. What Motown record label carried the slogan It's What's in the Groove That Counts?

A. Gordy Records.

Q. The one-hour crime show "Magnum, P.I." starred what Detroit native?

A. Tom Selleck.

Q. What famous television character was originated by Detroit-born actress Joyce Randolph (née Sirola)?

A. Trixie Norton (of "The Honeymooners").

Q. What Grand Rapids-born actor portrayed Tom Cudahy on "All My Children"?

A. Richard Shoberg.

Q. "The Heat Is On," from the film *Beverly Hills Cop*, was written by what Detroit-born musician?

A. Glen Grey.

Q. What was the original name of Michigan native Stevie Wonder?

A. Steveland Morris.

———◆———

Q. Long-time Detroit radio personality Harvey Ovshinsky wrote and produced what 1987 television Christmas tale?

A. "Santa Claus Is Alive and Well and Living in Detroit."

———◆———

Q. Bear Cave, situated just north of Buchanan, served as a setting for a portion of what movie?

A. *Train Robbery*.

———◆———

Q. What song written and produced by Motown's Berry Gordy was his first number one rhythm and blues record?

A. "Lonely Teardrops."

———◆———

Q. What saxophonist formed his first band in Detroit in the early 1940s, only to leave it to accept a position with the Gene Krupa band?

A. Sam Donahue.

———◆———

Q. Where was magician Harry Blackstone, Jr., born?
A. Three Rivers.

———◆———

Q. What Detroit native had a national hit with the 1968 single "Journey to the Centre of the Mind"?

A. Ted Nugent.

Q. What Highland Park-born baritone saxophonist played with Benny Goodman, Maynard Ferguson, and Donald Byrd during the 1950s?

A. Park ("Pepper") Adams.

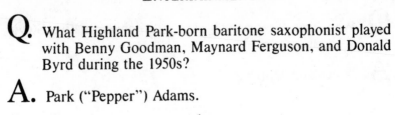

Q. What Detroit-born actor played opposite Stephanie Powers in the adventure series "Hart to Hart"?

A. Robert Wagner.

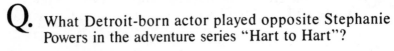

Q. What smash hit was recorded by the Flint-based group Question Mark and the Mysterians?

A. "Ninety-six Tears" (1966).

Q. What Big Band recording artist was born in Detroit on July 22, 1924?

A. Margaret Whiting.

Q. In what Michigan city was actor Lee Majors born?

A. Wyandotte.

Q. Jay Leno and Pat Morita starred in what 1987 action/comedy major motion picture filmed in Detroit?

A. *Collision Course.*

Q. What Detroit-born actor played Dr. Alexander Tazinski on the television medical drama "The Doctors and the Nurses"?

A. Michael Tolan.

Q. What sparkling jazz club is a part of the Historic Michigan Bean Company in Fenton?

A. It's the Raspberries Club.

◆

Q. Detroit native Marlo Thomas portrayed what character on the television comedy "That Girl"?

A. Ann Marie.

◆

Q. What internationally known singer/guitarist, born and raised in Detroit, first played in the band Last Heard?

A. Bob Seeger.

◆

Q. In what film did Pontiac-born drummer and combo leader Elvin Ray Jones have a drumming and acting role?

A. *Zachariah.*

◆

Q. What single record by the Supremes was their first to reach number one?

A. "Where Did Our Love Go?" (1964).

◆

Q. Michigan native Dennis Cole portrayed Detective Jim Briggs on what 1966–69 television crime show?

A. "Felony Squad."

◆

Q. What Detroit-born director–writer–producer won an Oscar for Best Screenplay for the 1970 movie *Patton?*

A. Francis Ford Coppola.

Q. Richard Pryor, Harvey Keitel, and Yaphet Kotto starred in what 1978 comedy/drama filmed in Detroit?

A. *Blue Collar.*

Q. What became the biggest single for Motown recording artist Jimmy Ruffin?

A. "What Becomes of the Broken Hearted?"

Q. What blues singer of the first half of this century is buried in the Coulter Chapel Cemetery in Cass County?

A. James Douglas Suggs.

Q. What Detroit native portrayed Dr. Maggie Powers on the television soap "The Doctors"?

A. Lydia Bruce.

Q. Under what name did Oliver Jackson and Eddie Locke perform in the Detroit area during the early 1950s?

A. Bob and Lock.

Q. What nickname was given to Michigan-born Big Band singer Johnny Desmond?

A. "The Creamer."

Q. What rock musician was born Vincent Furnier in Detroit on February 4, 1948?

A. Alice Cooper.

Q. For what instrument has Detroit-born Kenny Burrell gained first place recognition in such music polls as Japan's *Swing Journal*, London's *Melody Maker*, and *Ebony* magazine?

A. Guitar.

———◆———

Q. What character did Harry Morgan play from 1967 to 1970 in the television series "Dragnet"?

A. Bill Gannon.

———◆———

Q. What long-time member of the NBC "Tonight Show" orchestra was born in Detroit on June 13, 1938?

A. Ross Tompkins.

———◆———

Q. The Supremes had how many consecutive number one hits in 1964 and 1965?

A. Five.

———◆———

Q. Detroit-born James McGinnis changed his name and became a partner in what famous circus?

A. Barnum & Bailey Circus (James A. Bailey).

———◆———

Q. In what 1983 adventure film did Michigan-born Tom Selleck star with Bess Armstrong?

A. *High Road to China.*

———◆———

Q. In 1973 Kevin Toney became the leader of the Blackbyrds who earned a gold record with what first single release?

A. "Do It Fluid."

Q. What Detroit-born trombonist teamed up with Chuck Barris to compose theme music for several television series?

A. Michael Barone.

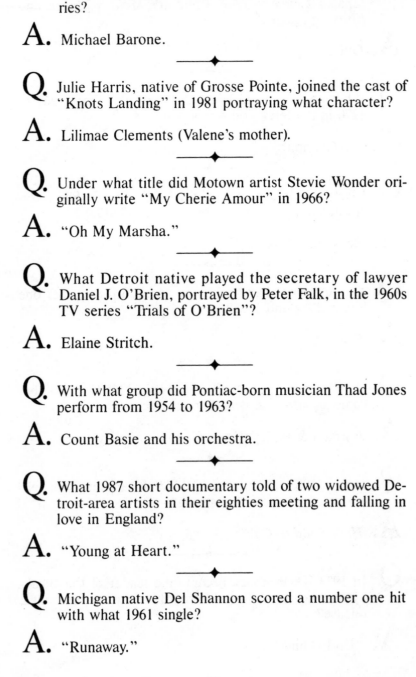

Q. Julie Harris, native of Grosse Pointe, joined the cast of "Knots Landing" in 1981 portraying what character?

A. Lilimae Clements (Valene's mother).

Q. Under what title did Motown artist Stevie Wonder originally write "My Cherie Amour" in 1966?

A. "Oh My Marsha."

Q. What Detroit native played the secretary of lawyer Daniel J. O'Brien, portrayed by Peter Falk, in the 1960s TV series "Trials of O'Brien"?

A. Elaine Stritch.

Q. With what group did Pontiac-born musician Thad Jones perform from 1954 to 1963?

A. Count Basie and his orchestra.

Q. What 1987 short documentary told of two widowed Detroit-area artists in their eighties meeting and falling in love in England?

A. "Young at Heart."

Q. Michigan native Del Shannon scored a number one hit with what 1961 single?

A. "Runaway."

Q. What 1959 motion picture filmed entirely in the Marquette area was the first movie shot "on location" in Michigan?

A. *Anatomy of a Murder.*

Q. In 1984 Sammy Davis, Jr., recorded a Motown salute to the Motor City by what title?

A. "Hello, Detroit."

Q. What was actress Piper Laurie's original name?

A. Rosetta Jacobs.

Q. Michigan native Danny Thomas starred as nightclub entertainer Danny Williams in what television sitcom?

A. "Make Room for Daddy" ("The Danny Thomas Show").

Q. The Four Tops from the North End section of Detroit enjoyed how many number one songs while recording for Motown?

A. Two ("I Can't Help Myself" and "Reach Out, I'll Be There").

Q. Battle Creek-born musician Melvin James ("Sy") Oliver served as arranger for what swing band during the 1940s?

A. Tommy Dorsey.

Q. Martha Reeves and the Vandellas officially disbanded on December 21, 1971, after a concert at what Detroit auditorium?

A. Cobo Hall.

Q. Motown's Berry Gordy established what record company on January 12, 1959, first releasing Mary Johnson's "Come to Me"?

A. Tamla Records.

———◆———

Q. What Detroit-born actor portrayed Sergeant Stan Wojehowicz ("Wojo") on television's "Barney Miller"?

A. Max Gail.

———◆———

Q. Who was the first voice of the "Green Hornet"?

A. Al Hodge (1936 to 1943).

———◆———

Q. Detroit's Smokey Robinson was the lead singer for what Motown group?

A. The Miracles.

———◆———

Q. Michigan-born actress Marlo Thomas had her first continuing role in what television sitcom?

A. "The Joey Bishop Show" (as Stella, Joey's sister).

———◆———

Q. What Detroit-born singer did the sound track for the 1972 CBS program, "Look Up and Live"?

A. Sheila Jordan (Sheila Dawson).

———◆———

Q. What Pontiac-born pianist worked as a staff musician at CBS for almost twenty years?

A. Henry ("Hank") Jones.

Q. Howard Keel co-starred with what Michigan-born actress in the 1950 film version of the Broadway play *Annie Get Your Gun?*

A. Betty Hutton.

---◆---

Q. Eddie Murphy portrayed a street-wise Detroit detective in what 1984 movie filmed in Detroit?

A. *Beverly Hills Cop.*

---◆---

Q. Michigan native Margaret Whiting recorded what highly successful ballad with trumpeter Billy Butterfield?

A. "Moonlight in Vermont."

---◆---

Q. Opening in 1899, what Detroit facility became one of the nation's big-time vaudeville theaters?

A. Temple Theater.

---◆---

Q. What Michigan company is the world's largest manufacturer of magic?

A. Abbot's Magic Manufacturing Company (in Colon).

---◆---

Q. Motown artists Diana Ross, Mary Wilson, and Florence Ballard rose to stardom from beginnings in what Detroit neighborhood?

A. Brewster Douglas Projects.

---◆---

Q. In what light adventure series did Detroit native Robert Wagner star as the suave crook Alexander Mundy?

A. "It Takes a Thief."

Q. What Detroit-born jazz trombonist and singer performed on the sound track of the movie *Hot Rock?*

A. Frank Rosolino.

Q. Michigan native Lee Majors starred as Heath Barkley in what ABC western series?

A. "The Big Valley."

Q. Dennis Quaid portrayed a country singer turned amateur prizefighter in what 1981 motion picture partially filmed in Detroit?

A. *Tough Enough.*

Q. Grand Rapids native Kim Zimmer portrayed what character on the television soap "The Doctors"?

A. Nola Dancy Aldrich.

Q. Motown's Brenda Holloway, along with Berry Gordy, penned what song in 1967 that later became a hit for Blood, Sweat & Tears?

A. "You've Made Me So Very Happy."

Q. What Traverse City native played Dr. Amos Wetherly on the television series "House Calls"?

A. David Wayne.

Q. What Detroit-born drummer formed the rock group Cool-Aid Chemists?

A. Paul Humphrey.

Q. What 1960s Detroit-based white-soul group scored hits with Little Richard's songs "Devil with a Blue Dress On" and "Good Golly, Miss Molly"?

A. Mitch Ryder and the Detroit Wheels.

Q. Motown's Tammi Terrell produced what single solo album of her career in 1968?

A. "I Can't Go On Without You."

Q. What character did Michigan-born Lee Majors play in the adventure series "The Fall Guy"?

A. Colt Seavers (Hollywood stuntman).

Q. What Detroit-born actor starred in the 1982 movie *Fighting Back?*

A. Tom Skerrit.

Q. Michigan native Ellen Burstyn won a Tony Award for what 1975 Broadway play?

A. *Same Time Next Year.*

Q. What Motown artist recorded "It Takes Two" with Marvin Gaye in 1966?

A. Kim Weston.

Q. Michigan native Ed McMahon first teamed with Johnny Carson on what ABC daytime show?

A. "Who Do You Trust?" (1958–1962).

Q. In what movie did Madonna receive her first major starring role?

A. *Desperately Seeking Susan.*

———◆———

Q. Pete Porter was the character portrayed by Detroit native Harry Morgan in what two television sitcoms?

A. "December Bride" and "Pete and Gladys."

———◆———

Q. Jazz singer Denise ("Dee Dee") Bridgewater grew up in what Michigan city?

A. Flint.

———◆———

Q. What is Sonny Bono's real name?

A. Salvatore Bono.

———◆———

Q. Detroit native Gilda Radner won a 1978 Emmy for her supporting role in what television series?

A. NBC's "Saturday Night Live."

———◆———

Q. What 1964 Motown release became Mary Wells's first and only number one song?

A. "My Guy."

———◆———

Q. What 1988 motion picture filmed in the Detroit area told the tale of two contemporary astronauts confronting the enemy Kaalium?

A. *Moontrap.*

Q. Spencer Tracy starred with what Port Huron native in the widely acclaimed 1933 film *The Power and the Glory?*

A. Colleen Moore.

Q. Della Rogers, an operator of a traveling snack stand on "Chico and the Man," was played by what Detroit-born singer?

A. Della Reese.

Q. What Motown release was the first to reach number one in both the pop and rhythm and blues charts?

A. "Please Mr. Postman" (sung by the Marvelettes, 1961).

Q. John Belushi portrayed a muckraking Chicago newspaper reporter in what 1981 Michigan-filmed motion picture?

A. *Continental Divide.*

Q. Robin Williams co-starred with what Detroit native in the TV sitcom "Mork & Mindy"?

A. Pam Dawber.

Q. At age thirteen Stevie Wonder had his first Motown hit by what title?

A. "Fingertips (Part 2)."

Q. What Detroit-born musician played the role of John Lennon in the road show of *Beatlemania?*

A. Marshall Crenshaw.

Q. In what 1950s kids' program did Detroit native Ed McMahon make his first national television appearance?

A. "Big Top" (appeared regularly as clown and strongman Dan Luri).

Q. Where was blues and jazz singer Beverly Jean ("Big Mama Bev") Hill born on January 6, 1938?

A. Birmingham.

Q. What Detroit native co-hosted the fast-moving comedy series "Laugh-In" with Dan Rowan?

A. Dick Martin.

Q. Ferndale native Dana Elcar portrayed Major ("Pappy") Boyington's commanding officer Colonel Lard in what World War II adventure series?

A. "Baa Baa Black Sheep."

Q. What actress who was born in Detroit on January 26, 1925, starred in the 1944 World War II film *Hollywood Canteen?*

A. Joan Leslie.

Q. What vocalists from Inkster became Motown's first female group?

A. The Marvelettes.

Q. What Grand Rapids-born actress played Roz in the 1980 movie *Nine to Five?*

A. Elizabeth Wilson.

Q. Drummer William McKinney directed what ten-piece swing band at the Arcadia Ballroom in Detroit during the late 1920s and early 1930s?

A. Cotton Pickers.

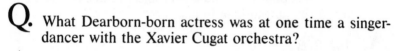

Q. What publishing company has published most of Motown's hits throughout the years?

A. Jobete Publishing.

Q. What 1988 movie filmed partially in Flint told the story of a brilliant black Detroit high school dropout who impersonated his way into many varied jobs?

A. *Chameleon Street.*

Q. What Dearborn-born actress was at one time a singer-dancer with the Xavier Cugat orchestra?

A. Adele Mara.

Q. In what 1984 film did Detroit native Lily Tomlin play a wealthy spinster co-starring with Steve Martin?

A. *All of Me.*

Q. On what record did Motown first use sound effects?

A. "I Wish It Would Rain" (by the Temptations, 1967).

Q. Detroit-born actor Richard Kiel played casino employee Moose Moran in what ABC television western?

A. "Barbary Coast."

Q. Little Stevie Wonder made his film debut in what 1964 films?

A. *Muscle Beach Party* and *Bikini Beach*.

Q. Detroit-born bass guitarist Major Quincy Holley, Jr., is known by what nickname?

A. "Mule."

Q. Benton Harbor-born musician William R. ("Bill") Berry was a member of what television show band?

A. "The Merv Griffin Show."

Q. What 1978 Detroit-filmed movie based on a Harold Robbins novel portrayed the power and intrigue of the wealthy in the automobile industry?

A. *The Betsy*.

Q. What veteran of many bebop groups was born in Detroit on March 16, 1930?

A. Tommy Lee Flanagan.

Q. What great singer often billed as the "Queen of the Blues" died from an overdose of sleeping pills in Detroit in 1963?

A. Dinah Washington.

Q. What Muskegon native directed the 1967 John Wayne–Kirk Douglas movie *The War Wagon?*

A. Burt Kennedy.

HISTORY

C H A P T E R   T H R E E

Q. In 1870 Detroit telephone customers became the first in the nation to have what type of reference information assigned to them?

A. Telephone numbers.

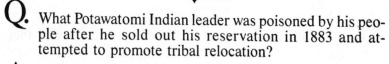

Q. From whose initials was the Reo Motor Car Company's name derived?

A. Ransom Eli Olds.

Q. What Potawatomi Indian leader was poisoned by his people after he sold out his reservation in 1883 and attempted to promote tribal relocation?

A. Chief Sawauquette.

Q. What political party was formed at a convention held in Jackson in July of 1854?

A. Republican Party.

Q. On February 4, 1902, what internationally famous aviation pioneer was born at 1120 W. Forest Avenue in Detroit?

A. Charles A. Lindbergh.

Q. In 1824 Congress appropriated money to survey what Detroit to Chicago roadway?

A. The Great Sauk Trail.

———◆———

Q. Who named Lake Saint Clair (Sainte Claire) in August of 1679?

A. Sieur de La Salle.

———◆———

Q. On March 29, 1929, Michigan became the first state in the nation to enact laws governing what explosive product?

A. Fireworks.

———◆———

Q. What house overlooking Harrisville Harbor was built by lumber baron George Colwell and today serves as a bed and breakfast facility?

A. The Widow's Watch.

———◆———

Q. What Michigan university dating back to the mid-1800s was formerly called the Michigan State Normal School?

A. Eastern Michigan University.

———◆———

Q. In 1987 what new source of transportation opened in downtown Detroit?

A. The Detroit People Mover.

———◆———

Q. What wealthy industrialist served as Holland's first mayor?

A. Isaac Cappon.

Q. Turn-of-the-century Ypsilanti resident Shelly M. Hutchinson helped develop and promote what retail marketing concept?

A. Trading stamps.

Q. What building near the Henry Ford Airport became the world's first airport hotel in 1931?

A. The Dearborn Inn.

Q. Michigan established a state lottery in what year?

A. 1972.

Q. What priest established the first "regular" mission at Keweenaw Bay in 1660?

A. Father Claude Allouez.

Q. When the first stretch of the Detroit & Pontiac Railroad was opened in 1838, what mode of locomotion was used to pull the railroad cars?

A. Horses.

Q. When granted a city charter by the legislature on May 8, 1907, what was the smallest "city" in Michigan?

A. East Lansing.

Q. What famous Civil War general and later U.S. president lived on East Fort Street in Detroit from April of 1849 to May of 1850?

A. Ulysses S. Grant.

Q. What steamboat that arrived at Detroit on August 27, 1818, was the first on the Upper Great Lakes?

A. *Walk-in-the-Water.*

———◆———

Q. What underwear manufacturing concern opened at Centerville in 1878?

A. Dr. Denton Sleeping Garment Mills.

———◆———

Q. Who in 1618 became the first European to set foot at the site of Sault Sainte Marie?

A. Etienne Brulé.

———◆———

Q. During the 1920s and 1930s, what mob was the most notorious on the Detroit crime scene?

A. The Purple Gang.

———◆———

Q. On what date did the Stars and Stripes fly for the first time over Michigan soil?

A. July 11, 1796.

———◆———

Q. Who became head administrator of the Battle Creek Sanitarium in 1876?

A. Dr. John Harvey Kellogg.

———◆———

Q. What was the estimated Indian population of Michigan when the first European explorers arrived in the early 1600s?

A. Approximately 15,000.

Q. Who established a fur-trading post on Mackinac Island in 1817?

A. John Jacob Astor.

———◆———

Q. What portion of Michigan's work force was unemployed in January of 1935?

A. One-fifth.

———◆———

Q. On March 6, 1896, what Detroit engineer became the first to test a motorized "horseless carriage" on the streets of Detroit?

A. Charles Brady King.

———◆———

Q. The nation's second continuously operated electric street railway system was opened in what Michigan city in 1886?

A. Port Huron.

———◆———

Q. Who built the first rooming house for college students in East Lansing during the late 1850s?

A. Joel Harrison.

———◆———

Q. At what 1876 event did furniture manufactured in Grand Rapids first gain national prominence?

A. The Philadelphia Centennial Exposition.

———◆———

Q. Following the capture of Mackinac Island by British forces during the War of 1812, what new name was given to Fort Holmes?

A. Fort George.

Q. Chronologically, where does Michigan rank among states in joining the union?

A. Twenty-sixth.

———◆———

Q. On what automotive line did the first electric starter appear in 1912?

A. Cadillac.

———◆———

Q. What organization modeled somewhat after the Ku Klux Klan, operated in Michigan under the pseudonym of the Wolverine Republican League during the 1930s?

A. The Black Legion.

———◆———

Q. Brick brought in from Saint Louis was used by Alby Rossman to build what 1863 structure in Allegan?

A. The Winchester Inn.

———◆———

Q. What world religious leader visited Detroit in 1987?

A. Pope John Paul II.

———◆———

Q. In what year did the Michigan state capital move to Lansing?

A. 1847.

———◆———

Q. What ambitious automotive pioneer organized General Motors Company in September of 1908?

A. William Crapo Durant.

Q. Who passed through the Straits of Mackinac in 1634 while looking for a passage to the Orient?

A. Jean Nicolet.

Q. Development of what canal connecting Lake Michigan and Lake Saint Clair was begun in 1838?

A. The Clinton and Kalamazoo.

Q. Built in 1857, what is the oldest home in Saugatuck?

A. The Park House (Horace D. Moore homestead).

Q. What signer of the Lewis Cass Treaty of 1819 is buried in Bay City?

A. Chief Ogemakegate.

Q. What Michigan university was the first state-supported university in the nation?

A. The University of Michigan in Ann Arbor.

Q. In 1904 the opening of what firm marked the beginning of the automobile manufacturing industry in Flint?

A. Buick Motor Company.

Q. What Michigan county courthouse was won in an 1880s poker game?

A. The Iron County Courthouse.

Q. On August 20, 1920, what commercial radio station became the first to broadcast daily scheduled programming in Michigan?

A. WWJ (Detroit).

Q. What annual licensing fee was charged to Michigan automobile owners in 1905 to operate their vehicles?

A. Fifty cents.

Q. What historic structure in Marshall was originally built in 1835 as a stagecoach stop?

A. The National House Inn.

Q. By 1910, how many miles of railroad tracks existed in Michigan?

A. 9,021.

Q. Who was the last chief of the Marquette Chippewa Indians?

A. Charles Kaw-Baw-Gam.

Q. Founded in Cass County in 1837, what was the first black church in Michigan?

A. Chain Lakes First Baptist Church.

Q. In 1925 Maxwell Motor Corporation was reorganized to form what company?

A. Chrysler Corporation.

Q. What unflattering title was given by locals to the firm of Smith, Tanner and Company who controlled the Lake Huron community of Forester in the 1870s?

A. "Ketchem, Skinem and Tannem."

Q. Detroit native Fred Sanders is credited with having invented what refreshing taste treat in 1875?

A. The ice cream soda.

Q. Whom did Henry Ford marry on April 11, 1888?

A. Clara Bryant.

Q. In 1788 Lord Dorchester, governor general of Canada, placed Michigan in what newly created judicial district?

A. District of Hesse.

Q. During the 1830s and 1840s, what was the approximate price paid in Detroit land offices for the timber-rich Saginaw Valley lands?

A. $1.50 per acre.

Q. In 1913 approximately how many automobiles were registered in Michigan?

A. 60,000.

Q. Constructed in 1836, what is the oldest commercial building in Saint Clair?

A. Murphy Inn.

Q. What South African leader drew record crowds during his 1986 visit to Detroit?

A. Bishop Desmond Tutu.

———◆———

Q. Niles was the birthplace of what two brothers of pioneer automotive fame?

A. Horace D. and John F. Dodge.

———◆———

Q. What public facility built between 1928 and 1930 became the world's first underwater tunnel for vehicles constructed between two countries?

A. The Detroit–Windsor Tunnel.

———◆———

Q. In 1841 what was the average per bushel price of wheat in Michigan?

A. Seventy cents.

———◆———

Q. The popularity and demand for Elijah McCoy's 1872 Automatic Machine Lubricator over imitation products is said to have spawned what phrase?

A. "The real McCoy."

———◆———

Q. What denomination relocated its printing house and headquarters to Battle Creek in 1855?

A. Seventh Day Adventists.

———◆———

Q. What type of small ship, designed to combat submarines, was built by Ford at the River Rouge facility in Dearborn during World War I?

A. "Eagle Boats."

Q. In 1950 what Detroit native became the first black man to win the Nobel Peace Prize?

A. Dr. Ralph Bunche.

━━━━━◆━━━━━

Q. Through what automotive enterprise was William Durant able to gain overwhelming control of General Motors in 1915?

A. Chevrolet Motor Company.

━━━━━◆━━━━━

Q. Who in 1805 became the first territorial governor of Michigan?

A. General William Hull.

━━━━━◆━━━━━

Q. Constructed in 1679 by Robert Cavelier, Sieur de La Salle, what was the first sailing vessel to ply the waters of the Great Lakes?

A. *Griffon*.

━━━━━◆━━━━━

Q. Who was the leader of the Mormons on Beaver Island from 1850 to 1856?

A. James Jesse Strang.

━━━━━◆━━━━━

Q. What conflict between the Menominee and Chippewa Indians is commemorated at Menominee?

A. The Sturgeon War.

━━━━━◆━━━━━

Q. What Russian exile came to Beaver Island in 1892 and provided free medical care to locals for the next thirty-three years?

A. Baron Perrot (Fedor Protar).

Q. What unusual religious colony was established by King Ben (Benjamin Franklin Purnell) in Benton Harbor in 1903?

A. The Israelite House of David.

---◆---

Q. During the panic of 1893 what was the medium of exchange in the "Thumb" area of Michigan?

A. Flour.

---◆---

Q. What young adventurer became the first Englishman to attempt to establish a mine in the mineral rich Keweenaw Peninsula area?

A. Alexander Henry.

---◆---

Q. What Detroit firm developed the paperboard milk carton during the 1930s?

A. Pure-Pak (Ex-Cell-O Corporation).

---◆---

Q. On what date did Henry Ford complete his first automobile?

A. June 4, 1896.

---◆---

Q. In 1806 what became the first bank to be established in Michigan?

A. The Bank of Detroit.

---◆---

Q. How many lives were lost in the November 3, 1926, Barnes–Hecker mines disaster in Marquette County?

A. Fifty-two.

Q. Produced in 1887, how many wheels did Ransom E. Olds's first horseless carriage have?

A. Three.

Q. What seventy-three-story facility opened in Detroit in 1977?

A. Renaissance Center.

Q. Built by Isaac Fairbanks in 1844 for the Rev. George N. Smith, what is the oldest historic landmark home in Holland?

A. Old Wing Inn.

Q. Under what treaty with Great Britain did France formally relinquish all of its holdings in North America, including the Michigan region, on February 10, 1763?

A. The Treaty of Paris.

Q. In 1903 what Farwell resident attempted to promote a large cement manufacturing venture that later closed because of inadequate funding?

A. Josiah L. Littlefield.

Q. To what British officer was Detroit surrendered on November 29, 1760?

A. Major Robert Rogers.

Q. For what amount did Henry Ford sell his first automobile?

A. Two hundred dollars.

Q. Often called the "black Lincoln," Frederick Douglass met with what notorious abolitionist of Harpers Ferry fame at Detroit in 1859?

A. John Brown.

———◆———

Q. What percentage of Fisher Body was purchased by General Motors in 1918?

A. Sixty percent.

———◆———

Q. In 1823 what Michigander became the first Catholic priest to serve in the U.S. Congress?

A. Father Gabriel Richard.

———◆———

Q. In what year was Lansing incorporated as a city?

A. 1859.

———◆———

Q. Who reputedly was the highest ranking Mafia leader in Detroit by the mid-1950s?

A. Joseph Zerilli.

———◆———

Q. By what name was Northern Michigan University first called when it was first established in Marquette in 1899?

A. Northern State Teachers' College.

———◆———

Q. Though not commercially successful when introduced around 1894 by Detroit jeweler and inventor George Schule, the "world's first" coffeemaker was called by what name?

A. Coffee Clock.

Q. Louis Campau, who helped settle the Grand Rapids area, received what nickname from the local Indians because of his wily trading?

A. "The Fox."

—◆—

Q. What Wayne tavern proprietor became the last person executed in Michigan prior to the abolishment of capital punishment by the state in 1846?

A. Stephen G. Simmons.

—◆—

Q. Because of what two residents of the 1830s did Marshall earn the title of "birthplace of the Michigan public school system"?

A. John D. Pierce and Isaac E. Crary.

—◆—

Q. In what year did Gerald R. Ford become president of the United States?

A. 1974.

—◆—

Q. What Indian tribe ceded Isle Royale to the federal government in 1842?

A. Ojibway.

—◆—

Q. In 1884 Kalamazoo acquired what mode of public transportation?

A. A horsecar line.

—◆—

Q. John P. Kolla established what manufacturing company in Holland in 1906?

A. The Holland Furnace Company.

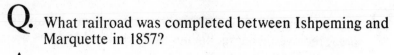

Q. What railroad was completed between Ishpeming and Marquette in 1857?

A. Iron Mountain Railroad.

Q. What is the oldest church structure in downtown Detroit?

A. Saints Peter and Paul Catholic Church (built around 1848).

Q. What copper baron financed the formation of Olds Motor Works in 1899?

A. S. L. Smith.

Q. Without having fired a single shot in defense, to whom did General William Hull surrender Detroit on August 16, 1812?

A. British General Brock.

Q. What great crusader against slavery and for economic competence and self-improvement of blacks lived in Battle Creek from 1858 until her death in 1886?

A. Sojourner Truth.

Q. Where in 1907 was the world's largest grey-iron foundry established?

A. Saginaw.

Q. On January 2, 1974, who was inaugurated as Detroit's first black mayor?

A. Coleman A. Young.

Q. What manufacturing firm was organized in 1899 with Henry Ford serving as chief engineer and manager?

A. The Detroit Automobile Company.

Q. For how many years following the Treaty of Paris on September 3, 1783, did the British continue to occupy portions of the Michigan region?

A. Thirteen.

Q. What famous Indian leader signed a peace treaty with the British at Detroit on August 17, 1765?

A. Pontiac.

Q. What was the first military outpost established in Michigan?

A. Fort de Buade (later called Fort Michilimackinac).

Q. Who was the first woman elected to the board of directors of the Greater Detroit Chamber of Commerce Board?

A. Esther Edwards (senior vice-president of Motown Records, 1973).

Q. How many Oldsmobiles were produced in 1901?

A. 425.

Q. What term was applied to the practice of sawmill owners' stealing unattended logs from a river as they were being floated to market during the early logging era in Michigan?

A. "Hogging."

Q. What Michigan city had its streets jammed with ice cakes during a flood in 1838?

A. Grand Rapids.

———◆———

Q. How many gallons of rum did the British provide the Indians at Detroit in 1779?

A. 17,520.

———◆———

Q. Between 1839 and 1845, the Wayne County Poorhouse for indigents and the insane was located in what Nankin Township facility?

A. The old Black Horse Tavern.

———◆———

Q. In the late summer of 1792, Detroit held its first election by selecting three representatives for what governing group?

A. The Parliament of Upper Canada.

———◆———

Q. What was the population of the Territory of Michigan in 1820?

A. 8,096.

———◆———

Q. The Reverend Isaac McCoy, the first Protestant missionary in western Michigan, founded what religious institution near Niles in 1822?

A. The Carey Mission.

———◆———

Q. During the American Revolution, what unflattering title was given to British governor Henry Hamilton by American patriots?

A. "The Hair Buyer of Detroit."

Q. On what date did the first Corvette, "America's only true production sports car," roll off the assembly-line in Flint?

A. June 30, 1953.

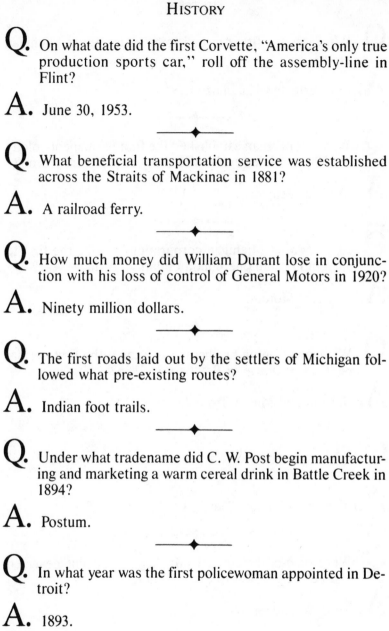

Q. What beneficial transportation service was established across the Straits of Mackinac in 1881?

A. A railroad ferry.

Q. How much money did William Durant lose in conjunction with his loss of control of General Motors in 1920?

A. Ninety million dollars.

Q. The first roads laid out by the settlers of Michigan followed what pre-existing routes?

A. Indian foot trails.

Q. Under what tradename did C. W. Post begin manufacturing and marketing a warm cereal drink in Battle Creek in 1894?

A. Postum.

Q. In what year was the first policewoman appointed in Detroit?

A. 1893.

Q. What Detroit native was refused a patent for an airplane in 1900 by a disbelieving U.S. Patent Office?

A. Hugo Mattulah.

Q. What was the first railroad to be chartered in Michigan in 1832?

A. The Erie and Kalamazoo.

Q. What Frenchman established the first permanent colony in 1790 that later evolved into the city of Port Huron?

A. Anselm Petit.

Q. In 1955 what Michigan corporation became the first to earn more than one billion dollars in a single year?

A. General Motors.

Q. What two trading brothers constructed the first permanent frame house in Bay City in 1836?

A. Joseph and Mader Tromble.

Q. What was the world's first urban freeway which was completed in 1942?

A. Davison Freeway (Detroit).

Q. What turn-of-the-century Muskegon resident designed and perfected the Continental motor?

A. Ross W. Judson.

Q. What was the nation's first black-owned television station, which began airing from Detroit in July of 1975?

A. WGPR/Channel 62.

Q. What public university, evolving out of several institutions of higher learning, was organized in Detroit in 1933?

A. Wayne State University.

———◆———

Q. What automotive line was started by Chrysler Corporation in 1928?

A. De Soto.

———◆———

Q. Who in 1824 was elected as Detroit's first mayor?

A. John R. Williams.

———◆———

Q. During the 1850s what Beaver Island community became the seat of Emmet County?

A. Saint James.

———◆———

Q. During the 1830s who opened the first orphanage in Michigan?

A. Father Martin Kundig.

———◆———

Q. What twenty-five-story brick and stone office tower was constructed in Lansing in 1931?

A. The Olds Tower.

———◆———

Q. The 1943 Detroit race riot, in which thirty-four people were killed, brought about what organization to handle racial problems in that city?

A. The Interracial Relations Committee.

Q. The capture of what Michigan fort on February 12, 1781, by Don Eugene Poure brought about a one day annexation of the facility by Spain?

A. Fort Saint Joseph.

———◆———

Q. From 1853 to 1855 the federal government constructed what canal around the falls of Saint Mary's?

A. The Soo Ship Canal.

———◆———

Q. The Michigan legislature established what watch dog group in 1921 to make recommendations for revisions in governmental activities?

A. Community Council Commission.

———◆———

Q. What gift of Andrew Carnegie became the first county library in Michigan in 1917?

A. The Port Huron (Saint Clair County) Public Library.

———◆———

Q. What was the name of Michigan's first trailer church, which began on October 1, 1937?

A. Saint Paul's Wayside Cathedral.

———◆———

Q. What British royalty arrived in Detroit on September 20, 1860?

A. Albert Edward, Prince of Wales (later King Edward VII).

———◆———

Q. On October 1, 1934, what Michigan institution of higher learning became the first in the nation to dispense with the system of grades, hours, credits, and points?

A. Olivet College.

Q. What P. T. Barnum-like clothing merchant became famous in Saginaw during the 1880s for his incredible merchandising exploits?

A. "Little Jake" Seligman.

Q. How many Detroiters participated in the June 23, 1963, "March for Freedom"?

A. 125,000.

Q. What Michigan native claimed to have made a seven-second flight in a power-driven, heavier-than-air craft at Saint Joseph Beach in October of 1898?

A. Augustus Moore Herring.

Q. Under what name was the University of Michigan established at Detroit in 1817?

A. Catholepistemiad (or University of Michigania).

Q. Following what 1937 event did Henry Ford finally grant his workers the right to join the United Auto Workers?

A. The Battle of the Overpass.

Q. Who was the first chamber of commerce president in Muskegon?

A. Newcomb McGraft.

Q. Originally built in 1848, the oldest hotel on Mackinac Island has what name?

A. The Island House Hotel.

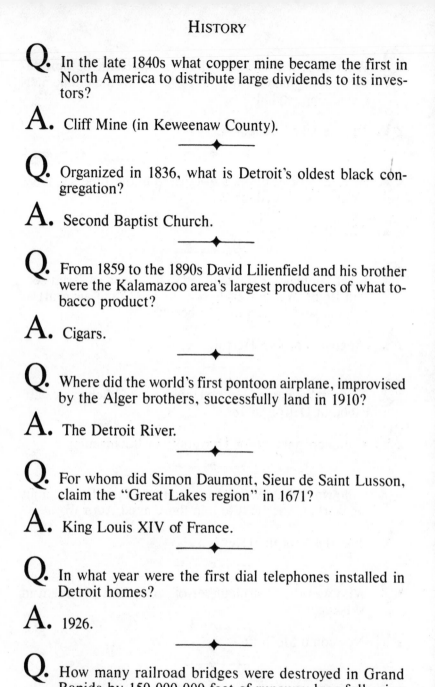

Q. In the late 1840s what copper mine became the first in North America to distribute large dividends to its investors?

A. Cliff Mine (in Keweenaw County).

Q. Organized in 1836, what is Detroit's oldest black congregation?

A. Second Baptist Church.

Q. From 1859 to the 1890s David Lilienfield and his brother were the Kalamazoo area's largest producers of what tobacco product?

A. Cigars.

Q. Where did the world's first pontoon airplane, improvised by the Alger brothers, successfully land in 1910?

A. The Detroit River.

Q. For whom did Simon Daumont, Sieur de Saint Lusson, claim the "Great Lakes region" in 1671?

A. King Louis XIV of France.

Q. In what year were the first dial telephones installed in Detroit homes?

A. 1926.

Q. How many railroad bridges were destroyed in Grand Rapids by 150,000,000 feet of runaway logs following heavy rains in 1883?

A. Three.

Q. In 1879 what amount was paid to the Campau family by the City of Detroit for Belle Isle?

A. $200,000.

Q. In 1930 where was the nation's first college accredited farriers' (blacksmith) course offered?

A. Michigan State University.

Q. In 1949 what Detroit automobile manufacturer became the first to produce more than one million passenger cars of one make in a one-year time period.

A. Chevrolet.

Q. In 1905 Governor Fred M. Warner signed a bill creating what much needed state agency?

A. Michigan State Highway Department.

Q. Funded by C. H. Hackley, where was the first monument dedicated in honor of President William McKinley following his 1901 assassination?

A. Muskegon.

Q. Who became the nation's first licensed chauffeur?

A. Henry Ford.

Q. What engineering marvel, opened for traffic in 1891, became the world's first electrified underwater tunnel in 1908?

A. The Port Huron–Sarnia Railway Tunnel.

Q. In 1866 what Detroit pharmacist introduced the world's first carbonated soft drink?

A. James Vernor (Vernor's ginger ale).

------◆------

Q. What facility for the visually impaired was opened in Lansing in 1880?

A. The Michigan School for the Blind.

------◆------

Q. Who organized the Lincoln Motor Car Company in 1917?

A. Henry M. Leland.

------◆------

Q. When was Michigan admitted into the union as a state?

A. January 26, 1837.

------◆------

Q. Branded on his right hand with the letters *S.S.* (for slave stealer) following his conviction for transporting slaves to freedom, what abolitionist is buried in the Muskegon Evergreen Cemetery?

A. Jonathan Walker.

------◆------

Q. The Burroughs Company, which was incorporated in Detroit in 1905, evolved out of what adding machine manufacturing firm?

A. American Arithomometer Company.

------◆------

Q. At what Detroit intersection was the world's first traffic light installed in 1915?

A. Woodward Avenue and Grand Avenue.

Q. What Michigan state department was established in 1921 with corrections, prison, welfare, institute, and hospital as its Commissions?

A. State Welfare Department.

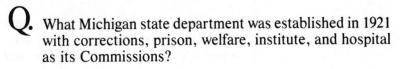

Q. More than a score of people lost their lives in what December of 1934 fire in Lansing?

A. The Hotel Kerns fire.

Q. Hazen S. Pingree, who served as mayor of Detroit from 1890 to 1901, initiated what innovative work relief program for the city's unemployed?

A. "Potato patches."

Q. What institute of higher learning authorized by the legislature in 1855 is the world's oldest agricultural college?

A. Michigan Agricultural College (Michigan State University).

Q. In 1893 what utility became available for home use in Detroit?

A. Electricity.

Q. What 21,000-seat facility opened in Detroit in 1979?

A. Joe Louis Arena.

Q. What firm was granted exclusive rights to oversee trade at Detroit on October 31, 1701?

A. The Company of the Colony of Canada.

Q. What lodging facility in Grand Marais was originally constructed in Seney in 1887 as a residence, only to be relocated later to its present site by the Manistique Railroad?

A. Lakeview Inn.

Q. What Detroit capitalist became president of Packard Motor Car Company in 1905?

A. Henry B. Joy.

Q. Who in 1668 founded the first permanent settlement in what later became the state of Michigan?

A. Father Jacques Marquette.

Q. What interdenominational society was organized in 1920 to "minister to the needs of the student body" at Michigan State?

A. The People's Church.

Q. How many sawmills were in operation in Michigan by 1849?

A. 558.

Q. What aviator made aviation history at Mount Clemens on October 14, 1922, by flying his plane beyond the 200 m.p.h. mark?

A. L. J. Maitland.

Q. In 1954 the nation's first shopping mall opened in what Detroit suburb?

A. Southfield (Northland Mall).

Q. In 1826 what turnpike was constructed between Port Huron and Detroit?

A. Fort Gratiot Turnpike.

Q. What unorthodox local church organized in Sturgis in 1858 introduced such innovations as motion pictures?

A. Free Church.

Q. In 1985 what commercial facility was opened in a former fur tannery in the Greektown district of downtown Detroit?

A. Trappers Alley.

Q. In 1871 the Michigan legislature allotted what sum of money for the construction of a new capitol building?

A. $1,200,000 (final cost $1,510,130).

Q. What national political convention was held at the Joe Louis Arena in Detroit in 1980?

A. Republican National Convention.

Q. What U.S. president signed the bill making Michigan a state?

A. Andrew Jackson.

Q. What name was applied to the "urban coalition" formed in Detroit following the civil disturbances in 1967?

A. "New Detroit."

Q. What religious movement met with persecution and violence in Northville in the early 1830s?

A. Methodism.

———◆———

Q. Where did Gerald R. Ford rank chronologically as president of the United States?

A. Thirty-eighth.

———◆———

Q. What keyboard instrument was patented by E. S. Votey of Detroit on May 22, 1900?

A. The pneumatic player piano.

———◆———

Q. December 10, 1915, marked what milestone in the production of Ford automobiles?

A. The millionth automobile.

———◆———

Q. In 1969 who became the first black person to be nominated for the office of mayor of Detroit?

A. Richard Austin.

———◆———

Q. In 1844 what fortification was established on the upper tip of the Keweenaw Peninsula?

A. Fort Wilkins.

———◆———

Q. In whose Detroit home did Michigan's first Jewish congregation conduct its first service on September 22, 1850?

A. Isaac and Sophie Cozens.

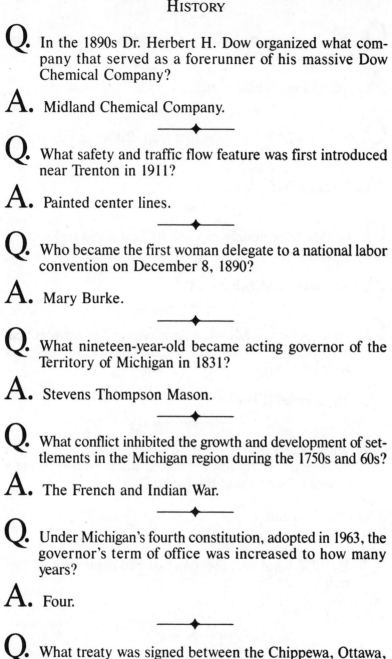

Q. In the 1890s Dr. Herbert H. Dow organized what company that served as a forerunner of his massive Dow Chemical Company?

A. Midland Chemical Company.

Q. What safety and traffic flow feature was first introduced near Trenton in 1911?

A. Painted center lines.

Q. Who became the first woman delegate to a national labor convention on December 8, 1890?

A. Mary Burke.

Q. What nineteen-year-old became acting governor of the Territory of Michigan in 1831?

A. Stevens Thompson Mason.

Q. What conflict inhibited the growth and development of settlements in the Michigan region during the 1750s and 60s?

A. The French and Indian War.

Q. Under Michigan's fourth constitution, adopted in 1963, the governor's term of office was increased to how many years?

A. Four.

Q. What treaty was signed between the Chippewa, Ottawa, Potawatomi and Wyandot Indian tribes and General William Hull on November 17, 1807?

A. The Treaty of Detroit.

Q. What were the call letters of the first radio station in the Great Lakes area?

A. WHQ (on Mackinac Island).

———◆———

Q. In 1666 who became the first recorded white man to find copper in the Keweenaw Peninsula area?

A. Father Claude Allouez.

———◆———

Q. In 1824 what couple erected the first home in Lenawee County?

A. Musgrove and Abi Evans.

———◆———

Q. What Detroit physician, pharmacist, and pharmaceutical manufacturer established a small business in 1862 that grew into Parke, Davis & Company?

A. Dr. Samuel P. Duffield.

———◆———

Q. What 1836 Farmington Hills inn was purchased in 1924 by Henry Ford for his wife Clara, whom he first met at a square dance held at the facility?

A. Botsford Inn.

———◆———

Q. By 1750 what was the approximate population of Detroit?

A. 650.

———◆———

Q. Because of its production of war materials, Michigan received what nickname during World War II?

A. "Arsenal of Democracy."

ARTS & LITERATURE

C H A P T E R   F O U R

Q. Iron County native Carrie Jacobs Bond composed what song often performed at weddings?

A. "I Love You Truly."

———◆———

Q. Who sculpted Detroit's great outstretched arm and fist monument to boxing great Joe Louis?

A. Robert Graham.

———◆———

Q. What novel did Harriette Arnow finish after moving to a farm near Ann Arbor in 1950?

A. *The Dollmaker.*

———◆———

Q. Grand Rapids-born artist Frederick Stuart Church provided illustrations for what southern folk classic?

A. *Uncle Remus, His Songs and His Sayings.*

———◆———

Q. Who painted the satirical work *State Election of 1837?*

A. T. H. O. P. ("Alphabet") Burnham.

Q. Known for his paintings of American Indian subjects, Eanger Irving Couse was born in what Michigan city on September 3, 1866?

A. Saginaw.

Q. What Michigan community is noted for its magnificent thirty-five-bell German carillon?

A. Frankenmuth.

Q. What 1850s Beaver Island resident wrote *A Child of the Sea* and *Life among the Mormons?*

A. Elizabeth Whitney Williams.

Q. What was the first professional theater in Michigan?

A. The National (Detroit, built in 1849).

Q. What Benzonia artist and poet has become internationally known for her linoleum block prints?

A. Gwen Frostic.

Q. What presidential library was established in Ann Arbor in 1981?

A. The Gerald R. Ford library.

Q. What Hanover attraction features an outstanding display of priceless reed organs?

A. Lee Conklin Antique Organ Museum.

Q. Established in 1900, what was Dearborn's first newspaper?

A. *Dearborn Independent.*

Q. Chandeliers in the hallway of the state capitol were crafted by what noted design firm?

A. Tiffany & Company.

Q. What world-renowned fine arts center is in Grand Traverse County?

A. Interlochen Center for the Arts.

Q. Former governor Chase S. Osborn published what novel in 1919?

A. *The Iron Hunter.*

Q. What was the first keyboard instrument in Michigan, arriving in Detroit in 1796?

A. A harpsichord.

Q. What ecologically functional piece of sculpture designed by Joseph Kinnevrew IV is on display at the Sixth Street Dam on Grand River in Grand Rapids?

A. Fish Ladder Sculpture.

Q. Michigan-born ceramic artist Mary Chase Stratton, along with Horace J. Caulkins, founded what pottery firm in 1904?

A. Pewabic Pottery Company.

Q. What Owosso-born painter became famous for his use of brilliant colors and for his ability to render sunlight?

A. Frederick Carl Frieseke.

———◆———

Q. What Victorian-style opera house in Coldwater is home to summer stock productions?

A. Tibbits Opera House.

———◆———

Q. In what year was the Muskegon Museum of Art founded?

A. 1912.

———◆———

Q. What early nineteenth-century artist received five dollars for designing Detroit's first city seal?

A. James Otto Lewis.

———◆———

Q. What poem did Henry Wadsworth Longfellow pen after reviewing Rowe Schoolcraft's works about the Indians of Michigan?

A. *"Hiawatha."*

———◆———

Q. What organization became Michigan's first "little theater" group in 1914?

A. The Ypsilanti Players.

———◆———

Q. The Poetry Resource Center of Michigan has headquarters in what community?

A. Royal Oak.

Q. What black poet of Cass County penned "To Be Negro in a Day like This"?

A. James David Corrothers.

———◆———

Q. Composer Leo Sowerby, who produced such works as *From the Northland, Prairie,* and *American Rhapsody,* was born in what Michigan city in 1895?

A. Grand Rapids.

———◆———

Q. What was Michigan playwright Paul Osborn's first play?

A. *The Vinegar Tree.*

———◆———

Q. Noted Michigan portrait and genre painter Percival Ives became dean of what art institution in 1890?

A. Detroit Museum of Art School.

———◆———

Q. What writer of outdoor stories was born in Owosso in 1878?

A. James Oliver Curwood.

———◆———

Q. Opened in 1885, what was the first theater in Grand Rapids to boast of electric lights, folding seats, and steam heat?

A. Smith's Opera House.

———◆———

Q. Who was considered Michigan's foremost artist from 1900 to 1930?

A. Gari Melchers.

Q. What director evolved the "permanent set" concept while working in theater in Detroit during the first World War?

A. Sam Hume.

———◆———

Q. Best remembered for his 1897 *Story of Ab*, what was University of Michigan graduate Stanley Waterloo's last work?

A. *Son of the Ages.*

———◆———

Q. What Michigan community was home to great American poet Carl Sandburg for several years?

A. Harbert.

———◆———

Q. What nationally syndicated public radio show is hosted by Dick Estelle of Michigan State University?

A. "From the Bookshelf."

———◆———

Q. What arts center featuring an open-air amphitheater is in the Manistee National Forest?

A. Blue Lake Fine Arts Camp.

———◆———

Q. Who designed the Scott Memorial Fountain on Belle Isle in 1925?

A. Cass Gilbert.

———◆———

Q. In 1910 what Michigan institution of higher learning became the first in the Midwest to establish an art history department?

A. University of Michigan.

Q. What was the title of Ernest Hemingway's first book, which was set in Michigan and published in 1923?

A. *Three Stories and Ten Poems.*

———◆———

Q. What attraction in Acme features a collection of automated musical instruments and a huge Belgian dance organ?

A. The Music House.

———◆———

Q. What 1925 novel by G. D. Eaton is considered to be a milestone in American realism?

A. *Backfurrow.*

———◆———

Q. Between 1870 and 1890 the shop of what noted Detroit woodcarver produced hundreds of wooden Indians?

A. Julius Melchers.

———◆———

Q. What stock theater director established the Civic Players of Detroit in 1928?

A. Jessie Bonstelle.

———◆———

Q. The Sanilac Petroglyphs may be viewed in what Michigan state park?

A. Port Crescent State Park.

———◆———

Q. *Lady Billy, Cornered,* and *The Scarlet Woman* were all penned by what Michigan playwright?

A. Zelda Sears.

Q. What Michigan poet made famous the line "It takes a heap o' living to make a house a home"?

A. Edgar Albert Guest.

Q. The Saginaw Art Museum is housed in what building?

A. The Ring Mansion.

Q. Holland author Arnold Mulder was best known for what 1921 work?

A. *The Sand Doctor.*

Q. What theatre in the Upper Peninsula built in 1900 has hosted such greats as Sarah Bernhardt and Douglas Fairbanks, Sr.?

A. Calumet Theatre.

Q. In 1979 former President Gerald R. Ford published his autobiography by what title?

A. *A Time to Heal.*

Q. What song was written by Gus Edwards in honor of Ransom E. Olds and his vehicle?

A. "In My Merry Oldsmobile."

Q. What University of Michigan library is recognized for its collection of original Revolutionary War documents?

A. William L. Clements Library.

Q. What Michigan poet, noted for his humorous ditties during the last half of the nineteenth century, penned "If I Should Die Tonight"?

A. Ben King.

———◆———

Q. Situated in Saugatuck, what is the third oldest summer stock theater in Michigan?

A. Red Barn Playhouse.

———◆———

Q. What noted topographer and railroad engineer in 1820 executed a painting of the steamship *Walk-in-the-Water* with Detroit in the background?

A. George Washington Whistler.

———◆———

Q. Under what pen name did early twentieth-century writer Ray Stannard Baker often write?

A. David Grayson.

———◆———

Q. In 1971 Simon and Schuster published what book containing the works of Michigan's "farmer–poet" Stillman J. Elwell?

A. *Windows of Thought*.

———◆———

Q. Grosse Pointe Farms author Marianne Shock is head of what literary organization?

A. Romance Writers of America.

———◆———

Q. What "Star Trek" novel by Flint author Diane Carey was published in 1988?

A. *Star Trek: Final Frontier*.

Q. Weauetonsin-born author Tom Galt's book, *How the United Nation Works*, has been published in how many languages?

A. Eighteen.

Q. Where did columnist Chet Shafer headquarter his "non-essential organization," the Guild of Former Pipe Organ Pumpers?

A. Three Rivers.

Q. The William Bonifas Fine Arts Center is in what Upper Michigan community?

A. Escanaba.

Q. Petoskey native Bruce Catton won the Pulitzer Prize for history with what work?

A. *A Stillness at Appomattox.*

Q. What Michigan producer became internationally known as a theatrical set designer?

A. Norman Bel Geddes.

Q. What was the actual last name of nineteenth-century Michigan tragedian Lawrence Barrett.

A. Brannigan.

Q. Gari Melchers's murals *War and Peace* were originally produced for what occasion?

A. The World's Columbian Exposition.

Q. What two artists were the principals in the founding of the Detroit Art Academy?

A. Joseph Gies and Francis P. Paulus.

———◆———

Q. Erected as a tribute to author James MacGillivary, the Paul Bunyan statue may be seen in what Michigan town?

A. Oscoda.

———◆———

Q. Based on *Les Misérables*, what was nineteenth-century Michigan playwright Bronson Howard's first play?

A. *Fantine*.

———◆———

Q. In 1986 what book by Birmingham businessman Wiley Sword was nominated for the Pulitzer Prize?

A. *President Washington's Indian War*.

———◆———

Q. What composition by Ann Arbor-born composer Normand Lockwood was dedicated to the 1939 New York World's Fair?

A. "Out of the Cradle Endlessly Rocking."

———◆———

Q. At what community in Kalamazoo County did James Fenimore Cooper stay while collecting material for his work *Oak Openings?*

A. Schoolcraft.

———◆———

Q. The Michigan Women's Historical Center and Hall of Fame, featuring a gallery of Michigan women artists, may be enjoyed in what city?

A. Lansing.

Q. What Michigan writer became known as the official biographer of President Woodrow Wilson?

A. Ray Stannard Baker.

Q. What Michigan poet–bard created Stone Circle north of Elk Rapids for literary events and workshops?

A. Terry Wooten.

Q. What professional resident theater company of national fame is headquartered in Lansing?

A. Boarshead (Michigan Public Theatre).

Q. Where is Michigan's largest commercial print shop?

A. Ada (Amway Corporation).

Q. What contemporary Michigan author is known for such spy thrillers as *The Drakov Memoranda*, *The Caternary Exchange*, and *Berlin Fugue?*

A. J. C. Winters.

Q. What Ionia-born artist, who studied under Joseph Gies at the Detroit Museum Art School, became well known for his paintings of the peasantry and scenery of northern France?

A. Myron G. Barlow.

Q. What Michigan writer born in Muskegon in 1877 became known as the "Lumberman Poet"?

A. Douglas Malloch.

Q. What internationally renowned American poet taught at the University of Michigan from 1921 to 1923 and from 1925 to 1926?

A. Robert Frost.

Q. Where may over 200 artifacts hand-carved from white pine stumps and roots be seen?

A. Shrine of the Pines (in Baldwin).

Q. The Kresge Art Museum is on what Michigan campus?

A. Michigan State University.

Q. What poetry first for Detroit was held on June 17, 1988?

A. Pro–Am Open Poetry Reading.

Q. *Greenland Lies North* and *Lifeline through the Arctic* are both books by what Ironwood native?

A. William S. Carlson.

Q. What Michigan writer noted for such works as *Quest, The Surrey Family,* and *Islanders* received a Guggenheim Fellowship grant in 1931 in the field of creative writing?

A. Helen Rose Hull.

Q. The Detroit Board of Education introduced what new music curriculum to the local school system in 1917?

A. High-school orchestra.

Q. Where in Michigan did Illinois-born Ernest Hemingway spend many of his childhood summers?

A. Lake Walloon (near Petoskey).

Q. What 1940 novel by Iola Fuller that used Mackinac Island as its setting received the Hopwood Award?

A. *The Loon Feather.*

Q. What long-time Saugatuck resident was called the "best of the Greek poets in America"?

A. George Coutoumanos.

Q. In 1907 what organization became Michigan's first fellowship of artists?

A. The Hopkin Club (named in honor of Robert Hopkins).

Q. What Detroit painter died in 1894 before completing a commissioned portrait of President Grover Cleveland, only to have the work finished by his son Percy?

A. Lewis Thomas Ives.

Q. In 1881 the nation's first high-school music course was planned by Dr. Francis York for what Michigan city school system?

A. Ann Arbor.

Q. The practice of forest conservation was the subject of what 1922 novel by Harold Titus?

A. *Timber.*

Q. How tall is Ironwood's *Hiawatha*, the world's tallest statue of an Indian?

A. Fifty-two feet.

———◆———

Q. What nineteenth-century art teacher is credited with having produced the first glazed pottery in Detroit?

A. Ruth Beedzler.

———◆———

Q. What is the oldest continuously operating theater in Michigan?

A. The Croswell Opera House (in Adrian).

———◆———

Q. Where was Michigan author, poet, and artist Jean Stanbury Holden born in 1843?

A. Pinckney.

———◆———

Q. Who organized the first large orchestra in Michigan at Detroit in 1869?

A. Wilhelm Bendix.

———◆———

Q. What Michigan city is home for the Cherry County Playhouse?

A. Traverse City.

———◆———

Q. What 1923 novel by Michigan writer Will Levington Comfort has been called "one of the greatest elephant stories ever written"?

A. *Samadhi.*

Q. What internationally known cartoonist was born in Detroit on June 30, 1860?

A. Thomas May.

Q. Michigan poet Theodore Roethke received the Pulitzer Prize in 1954 for what collection of his works?

A. *The Waking.*

Q. Who designed the mansion and grounds of Cranbrook in Bloomfield Hills?

A. Albert Kahn.

Q. The works of what nationally known wildlife artist are displayed at the Iron County Museum in Caspian?

A. Lee Le Blanc.

Q. The Art Center of Battle Creek features how many galleries?

A. Four.

Q. What thirty-one-foot woven work of art is in the council chamber of the Bay City City Hall?

A. The Chmielewska Tapestry.

Q. Though unsuccessful in achieving their demands, the printers at the Detroit *Free Press* first struck in what year?

A. 1865.

Q. Where in Michigan may the world's largest musical fountain be enjoyed?

A. Grand Haven.

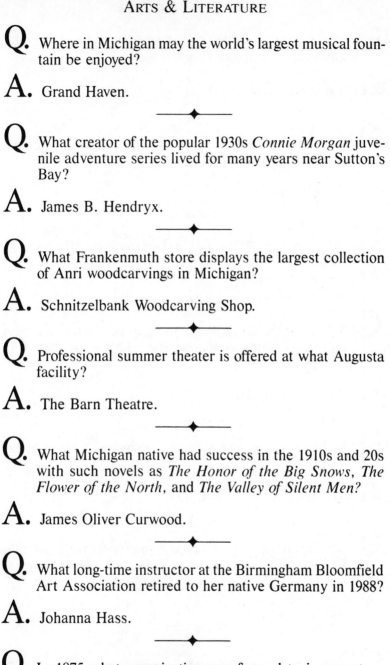

Q. What creator of the popular 1930s *Connie Morgan* juvenile adventure series lived for many years near Sutton's Bay?

A. James B. Hendryx.

Q. What Frankenmuth store displays the largest collection of Anri woodcarvings in Michigan?

A. Schnitzelbank Woodcarving Shop.

Q. Professional summer theater is offered at what Augusta facility?

A. The Barn Theatre.

Q. What Michigan native had success in the 1910s and 20s with such novels as *The Honor of the Big Snows, The Flower of the North,* and *The Valley of Silent Men?*

A. James Oliver Curwood.

Q. What long-time instructor at the Birmingham Bloomfield Art Association retired to her native Germany in 1988?

A. Johanna Hass.

Q. In 1875 what organization was formed to inaugurate a permanent art gallery in Detroit?

A. The Detroit Art Association.

Q. What 1934 novel by David Cornel DeJong was built around the theme of Dutch immigrants in Michigan?

A. *Belly Fulla Straw.*

------◆------

Q. Edgar Albert Guest went to work for what Michigan newspaper in 1895?

A. Detroit *Free Press.*

------◆------

Q. Who composed the symphony *After Walt Whitman?*

A. Eric DeLamarter.

------◆------

Q. What nineteenth-century Michigan playwright has been hailed by some critics as the "Father of American Drama"?

A. Bronson Howard.

------◆------

Q. In 1886 what chamber music group was formed in Detroit?

A. Detroit Philharmonic Club.

------◆------

Q. In 1852, what painter, noted for portraits of Major John Biddle and Governor Lewis Cass, became professor of fine arts at the University of Michigan?

A. Alvah Bradish.

------◆------

Q. The Grand Rapids Art Museum is housed in what 1879 building?

A. Grand Rapids' first federal building and post office.

Q. In 1913 what Fairfield-born painter became the first foreigner to be awarded the Gold Medal of the French Société des Artistes Français?

A. Lawton S. Parker.

Q. The history of the community of Frankenmuth is portrayed in images on the stained glass windows of what church?

A. Saint Lorenz (in Frankenmuth).

Q. What Michigan art facility features 101 galleries?

A. Detroit Institute of Arts.

Q. What Manistee theater was built around the turn of the century by a lumber magnate?

A. Ramsdell Theatre (by T. J. Ramsdell).

Q. In the late 1830s what became the first labor paper to be published in Michigan?

A. *Rat Gazette*.

Q. In what facility is the University of Michigan Museum of Art situated?

A. Alumni Memorial Hall.

Q. Who directed grand opera in association with the Detroit Civic Opera between 1928 and 1938?

A. Thaddeus Wronski.

Q. What Bellaire native became known as the "Frog Holler Poet"?

A. Max Ellison.

Q. Following World War I, what Grand Haven-born painter and etcher became director of the Carolina Art Association School?

A. Alfred Heber Hutty.

Q. In 1937 an orchestra comprised of what type of unique instruments made its debut in Detroit?

A. Tamburitzas.

Q. *Microbe Hunters, Hunger Fighters, Men Against Death*, and *The Fight for Life* are all medical science works by what Zeeland-born writer?

A. Paul de Kruif.

Q. What Labor Day weekend music festival is held in Detroit?

A. Montreux Detroit Jazz Festival.

Q. For what book was Michigan poet Robert Gressner best known?

A. *Upsurge.*

Q. What ethnic group is the subject of Leonard Cline's 1925 Michigan mining novel *God Head?*

A. Finns.

Q. At what lake near Ishpeming did Lewis H. Morgan collect data for his authoritative wildlife book *The American Beaver and Its Works?*

A. Mud.

Q. What two novels by Eugene Thwing were built around the uproarious lumber life of Midland County?

A. *The Man from Red Keg* and *The Red Keggers.*

Q. What arts and nature facility is between Niles and Saint Joseph?

A. Fernwood Arts and Crafts Botanic Gardens and Nature Center.

Q. Under what title was a collection of Detroit-born poet Chuck Kisandi's works published in 1984?

A. *Sobering Thoughts Plus Rambling Wit.*

Q. Who served as conductor of Detroit's first symphony orchestra from 1914 to 1918?

A. Weston Gales.

Q. *The Adventures of Paul Bunyan* was published in 1927 by what Marquette College professor?

A. James Cloyd Bowman.

Q. Bloomfield Hills author George Lee Walker wrote what 1985 "corporate life" novel?

A. *The Chronicles of Doodah.*

Q. What regional magazine was brought to Michigan in 1920 by John T. Frederick?

A. *The Midland.*

———◆———

Q. Who in 1855 created the first painting of the University of Michigan campus?

A. Jasper F. Cropsey.

———◆———

Q. A small, predominantly Scandinavian Upper Michigan lumber town during the Great Depression is the setting of what 1934 book by Mildred Walker?

A. *Fireweed.*

———◆———

Q. Where in Chassell may antique linotypes and printing presses be seen in operation?

A. The Printing Museum.

———◆———

Q. In what year was Michigan's first art exhibition held in Detroit?

A. 1852.

———◆———

Q. What work of Michigan poet Julia Moore was an overnight success when published in 1876 to honor the nation's centennial?

A. *The Sweet Singer of Michigan Salutes the Public.*

———◆———

Q. Who became the most noted leader among Michigan artists during the last half of the nineteenth century?

A. Robert Hopkin.

Q. Between 1868 and 1886 what portrait and scenic painter became well known in Detroit as a designer of flags and banners?

A. Adam Walthem.

---◆---

Q. Painter J. M. Stanley, who came to Michigan in 1824, is best known for painting what subject?

A. Indians.

---◆---

Q. The 1985 private eye adventure *Sugartown*, set in Detroit, was penned by what Whitmore Lake resident?

A. Loren D. Estleman.

---◆---

Q. What is Michigan's only year-round live theater?

A. Thunder Bay "Live" Theater.

---◆---

Q. During the 1830s and 40s what Michigan writer penned such works as *A New Home*, *Forest Life*, and *Western Clearings?*

A. Caroline Kirkland.

---◆---

Q. What Detroit organization developed out of the Hopkin Club to stimulate, promote, and guide artistic interests?

A. The Scarab Club.

---◆---

Q. What was the title of Douglas Malloch's book of verse that was first published in 1923?

A. *Come On Home*.

Q. During the 1930s, what Michigan native wrote of the industrial development of the State in such works as *Once a Wilderness* and *Second Growth?*

A. Arthur Pound.

Q. On June 22, 1804, what topographical painter and British surgeon produced a watercolor of the Detroit settlement?

A. Edward Walsh.

Q. Early twentieth-century Michigan writer Henry Alverson Franck was best known for books on what subject?

A. Travel.

Q. In 1981 what was Michigan writer Christian Kassel's first published western?

A. *Gum Gamble.*

Q. "Along Shore," "A Bit of Beach, Lake Superior," "A Ten Knot Breeze," and "A Bit of Shore," are works by what nineteenth-century, Detroit-born and educated artist?

A. Nathaniel C. Bullock.

Q. Novelist Gary Gildner was born in what Michigan community?

A. West Branch.

Q. In what 1908 novel by Steward Edward White is life in a lumber camp colorfully described?

A. *The Riverman.*

SPORTS & LEISURE

C H A P T E R   F I V E

Q. During the 1988 Summer Olympics in Seoul, Korea, what Homer resident became the first U.S. kayaker ever to win a gold medal?

A. Greg Barton.

◆

Q. What successful speedboat designer and racer was known as "the gray fox from Algonac, Michigan"?

A. Garfield Arthur Wood.

◆

Q. Who owned the Detroit Pistons prior to July 27, 1974, when a Detroit syndicate purchased the club?

A. Fred Zollner.

◆

Q. What Michigan ski facility is the home of the world's largest artificial ski jump?

A. Pine Mountain Ski–Jumping Complex (Iron Mountain).

◆

Q. Running on the ice of Lake Saint Clair, what Ford racer broke the mile speed record in 1904?

A. "999."

Q. Prior to his 1965 retirement, Detroit boxing great Ray ("Sugar Ray") Robinson won how many of his 202 professional fights?

A. 175.

---◆---

Q. What Michigan State University football player was the top punter in the nation in 1937?

A. John ("Johnnie") S. Pingel.

---◆---

Q. Oakland University in Rochester is a member of what athletic conference?

A. Great Lakes Intercollegiate.

---◆---

Q. What PGA-sanctioned event is held at Grand Blanc each July?

A. The Buick Open.

---◆---

Q. What years did Gordon ("Gordie") Howe play with the Detroit Red Wings?

A. 1946 to 1971.

---◆---

Q. Kirk Gibson set an individual record in 1984 with how many game-winning RBIs?

A. Seventeen.

---◆---

Q. By what nickname was Ewell Doak Walker II known when he played with the Detroit Lions from 1950 to 1955?

A. "The Doaker."

Q. What unique competition is held each year at the Tree-Mendus Fruit Farm, near Eau Claire?

A. The International Cherry Pit Spit Championship.

Q. At his retirement in 1965, who was the highest scoring left wing in the National Hockey League's history?

A. Robert ("Ted") B. Lindsay.

Q. What are the team colors of the Eastern Michigan University Hurons?

A. Dark green and white.

Q. The Bays de Noc in Escanaba offers what annual entertainment the third week in August?

A. The Upper Peninsula State Fair.

Q. What specialized area of athletics did Istvan J. Danosi skillfully coach at Wayne State University from 1956 to 1982?

A. Fencing.

Q. Where does Michigan rank internationally in the production of dogsleds?

A. First.

Q. What Michigan native is internationally known as the United States's foremost sponsor of amateur sports?

A. Michael Adray.

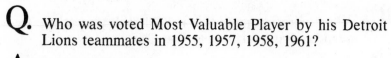

Q. Who was voted Most Valuable Player by his Detroit Lions teammates in 1955, 1957, 1958, 1961?

A. Joseph P. Schmidt.

Q. The Detroit Tigers took the 1984 World Series four games to one over what opponent?

A. San Diego Padres.

Q. What two communities share in hosting the National Asparagus Festival?

A. Shelby and Hart.

Q. Prior to 1933 what was the name of the National Hockey League franchise in Detroit?

A. The Falcons.

Q. During Matthew Mann's twenty-nine years as head swimming coach, he led the University of Michigan to how many Big Ten swimming titles?

A. Sixteen.

Q. Ishpeming is home to what national sports museum?

A. The U.S. National Ski Hall of Fame.

Q. What River Rouge High School coach led his teams to twelve state Class B Basketball championships?

A. Lofton C. Greene.

Q. Who is known as the "father of Michigan's Inter-scholastic Athletics"?

A. Charles E. Forsythe.

Q. Who became the first Tiger since Al Kaline (1955) to collect 200 hits and 100 RBIs in the same season?

A. Alan Trammell (1987).

Q. Where is the only ski flying hill in the Americas?

A. Copper Peak, Ironwood.

Q. Before becoming a football commentator on television, for how many years did Alexander ("Alex") Karras play with the Detroit Lions?

A. Twelve.

Q. What roller coaster made its debut during the 1988 season at Boblo Island amusement park?

A. "The Nightmare."

Q. What three playing fields occupied the site of Tiger Stadium before it was built?

A. Bennett Park (1900), Navin Field (1912), and Briggs Stadium (1938).

Q. Who was the three-time Olympic fencing champion from Wayne State University?

A. Paul Sweeney.

Q. What was the number of the jersey, now retired by the University of Michigan, that was worn by two-time All-American Ron Kramer?

A. 87.

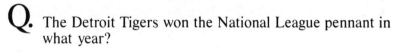

Q. The Detroit Tigers won the National League pennant in what year?

A. 1887.

Q. What firm at Silver Lake offers eight-mile rides over the surrounding scenic dunes?

A. Mac Wood's Dune Rides.

Q. What Harrisville-born Baseball Hall of Famer was named Hazen Shirley by his parents?

A. Kiki Cuyler.

Q. What outstanding Detroit Lions player wore the now-retired jersey number 37?

A. Ewell Doak Walker II.

Q. Where may one tour the last coal-burning, overnight passenger steamship to operate on the Great Lakes?

A. Douglas (the S.S. *Keewatin*).

Q. Elected to the Michigan Sports Hall of Fame in 1959, who is acclaimed as the greatest woman bowler of all time?

A. Marion Van Oosten Ladewig.

Q. How many times did Detroit Red Wings goaltender Terrance ("Terry") Gordon Sawchuk win the Vezina Trophy?

A. Three.

Q. What Michigan State basketball player won the Big Ten scoring championship in 1986?

A. Scott Skiles.

Q. How many consecutive Big Ten championships did Harry Kipke's University of Michigan football teams win?

A. Four.

Q. In how many World Series championships have the Detroit Tigers participated through the 1988 season?

A. Nine.

Q. What Detroit Lion set a Silverdome record on September 27, 1981, with a 74-yard punt?

A. Tom Skladany.

Q. What Frankenmuth attraction includes a 1920s version of Main Street U.S.A.?

A. Antique Auto Village.

Q. What Detroit native is the only pitcher in the major leagues to hurl two shutouts in a double header?

A. Ed Reulbach (Chicago Cubs, 1908).

Q. What middleweight boxing champion was known as the "Michigan assassin from Grand Rapids"?

A. Stanley Ketchel.

Q. Who is the only athlete in the University of Michigan's history to earn twelve varsity letters?

A. Peter ("Pete") Robert Elliott (1945 to 1949).

Q. What Benton Harbor/Saint Joseph extravaganza is Michigan's oldest spring celebration?

A. Blossomtime Festival.

Q. Who is known as the "father of scholastic wrestling in Michigan"?

A. Clifford ("Cliff") Patrick Keen.

Q. What Detroit Pistons player wore the now-retired number 21 jersey?

A. David Bing.

Q. How many consecutive batters did Detroit Tigers' pitcher Lynwood Thomas ("Schoolboy") Rowe retire during the 1934 World Series victory over Saint Louis?

A. Twenty-two.

Q. Who coached the Detroit Lions to their 1952 and 1953 world championships?

A. Raymond Klein ("Buddy") Parker.

Q. What Michigan State basketball player holds the record for most assists in a single season?

A. Earvin ("Magic") Johnson.

Q. Where was the nation's first and foremost championship billiards match held in 1858?

A. Detroit.

Q. What University of Michigan football and track star defeated fabled Jesse Owens at the sixty-yards and high hurdles in 1935?

A. Willis F. Ward.

Q. What Detroit Tiger was the first modern major leaguer to win the triple crown?

A. Ty Cobb (1909).

Q. Who founded the Michigan Sports Hall of Fame in 1955?

A. William Nicholas ("Nick") Kerbawy.

Q. On January 6, 1955, what Eastern Michigan basketball player set a school record for most free throws during a single game?

A. Andy Shepard (eighteen).

Q. What Detroit Tiger uniform numbers have been retired?

A. 5 (Hank Greenberg), 2 (Charlie Gehringer), and 6 (Al Kaline).

Q. Michigan golfer Albert Watrous, who turned pro in 1920, captured the Michigan Open how many times?

A. Six.

Q. In 1970 what Detroit high school basketball coach became the first black head basketball coach at a major university?

A. William ("Will") Joseph Robinson (Illinois State).

Q. During the 1968–69 season what Northern Michigan University basketball player set a school record for most points scored by an individual during a single game?

A. Ted Rose (54 against Central Michigan).

Q. What organization, which held its first ski-jumping competition at Ishpeming in February, 1888, is thought to be Michigan's first ski club?

A. Norden Ski Club.

Q. On what date did the Detroit Tigers play their first night game at Tiger Stadium?

A. June 15, 1948.

Q. On August 20, 1980, what Detroit Tiger combination completed a triple play against the Milwaukee Brewers?

A. Tom Brookens to Lou Whitaker to Richie Hebner.

Q. Who was voted the Detroit Lions' Most Valuable Player on offense for the 1987 season?

A. Pete Mandley.

Q. In 1988 what one-armed baseball pitcher from Flint won the much-coveted Sullivan award?

A. Jim Abbott.

———◆———

Q. What five-mile trek is sponsored by Saint Ignace and Mackinaw City each Labor Day?

A. The Mackinac Bridge Walk.

———◆———

Q. What celebration, in Detroit and Windsor encompassing both Dominion Day and Independence Day, exhibits freedom and friendship between the United States and Canada?

A. International Freedom Festival.

———◆———

Q. What is Michigan's second largest source of income?

A. Tourism.

———◆———

Q. During the early 1950s, what Detroit Lions player was known as "Hunchy"?

A. Robert J. Hoernschemeyer.

———◆———

Q. What Eastern Michigan University football coach holds the school's highest career win percentage?

A. Vernie S. Bennett (.714 in 1894).

———◆———

Q. What Detroit Tiger received the American League Most Valuable Player and the Cy Young Award in 1968?

A. Denny McLain.

Q. Where was George ("The Gipper") Gipp of Notre Dame football fame born?

A. Laurium, Michigan.

Q. Who in 1917 became Wayne State's first athletic director?

A. David Lynn Holmes.

Q. After Tiger Stadium was rebuilt in 1938, what major leaguer was the first to hit an over-the-roof home run?

A. Ted Williams (May 4, 1939, his rookie season).

Q. Where is the National Cherry Festival held each July?

A. Traverse City.

Q. Who coached the Detroit Lions to their 1952 and 1953 world championships?

A. David L. Holmes.

Q. What Fenton firm specializes in hot-air balloon rides and vacations?

A. Balloon Corporation of America.

Q. What is the name of the Detroit Tigers' spring training complex in Lakeland.

A. Tigertown.

Q. What U.S. ski jumping record was set at Pine Mountain in 1982?

A. 399 feet (by Austrian Armin Kogler).

Q. What former University of Michigan football star went on to play with the Detroit Lions and led that team in scoring with fifty-four points in 1945?

A. Robert ("Bob") Barton Westfall.

Q. During his twenty-six years in competition, what Michigan bowler and member of the National Bowlers Hall of Fame posted forty-two "300" games in sanctioned competition?

A. George L. Young.

Q. In addition to winning four national titles, Michigan super speed skater Jeanne Robinson Omelenchuk won how many North American titles during her career?

A. Six.

Q. With over 700,000 registered craft, Michigan ranks where nationally in total number of pleasure boats?

A. First.

Q. What 1949 Hall of Famer was the greatest second baseman ever to come out of the state of Michigan?

A. Charlie Gehringer.

Q. What years did Robert ("Ted") B. Lindsay play for the Detroit Red Wings?

A. 1944 to 1957 and 1964 to 1965.

Q. Where were the Pistons headquartered prior to moving to Detroit in 1957?

A. Fort Wayne, Indiana.

———◆———

Q. In 1934 what amount was paid by the Detroit Tigers' organization for catcher Mickey Cochrane?

A. $100,000.

———◆———

Q. How many members of the 1988 Detroit Lions team had previously played in the Great Lakes Conference?

A. Three: Paul Butcher, Jeff Chadwick, and Rob Rubick.

———◆———

Q. Who was the original "Iron Man" of the Detroit Tigers' pitching staff?

A. George Emmett Mullin (1902–13).

———◆———

Q. At what attraction near Flint may visitors ride on Michigan's only authentic steam-powered, narrow-gauge railroad?

A. Crossroads Village and Huckleberry Railroad.

———◆———

Q. Where is the Upper Peninsula Championship Rodeo held?

A. Iron River.

———◆———

Q. How many times did Joe Louis (Barrow) successfully defend his world heavyweight boxing title?

A. Twenty-five.

Q. What is the largest motor speedway in Michigan?

A. Michigan International Speedway (Brooklyn).

———◆———

Q. In what year did Garfield A. Wood, the world's "King of Speed" on water, first win the coveted Harmsworth Trophy from England?

A. 1920.

———◆———

Q. What member of the Michigan Sports Hall of Fame is said to have dominated the world of golf from 1914 to 1936?

A. Walter C. Hagen.

———◆———

Q. The University of Michigan defeated what team, 49–0, in the first Tournament of Roses game?

A. Stanford.

———◆———

Q. What baseball personality became the first manager to win a World Series in both leagues?

A. Sparky Anderson.

———◆———

Q. Holder of the Lightweight Boxing Championship title from 1910 to 1912, Adolph ("Ad") A. Wolgast was born in what Michigan city?

A. Cadillac.

———◆———

Q. What Michigan State University football player held the NCAA pass interception yards return record for twenty-four years?

A. Lynn Everett "Chad" Chandnois (1946–49).

Q. Who teamed with Alan Trammell as the Tigers' double play duo for a Major League record tenth straight season in 1987?

A. Lou Whitaker.

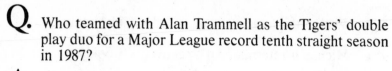

Q. What facility serves as home court for the Eastern Michigan University basketball team?

A. Bowen Field House.

Q. What individual is credited with establishing hockey as a major league sport in Detroit?

A. John J. Adams.

Q. What professional baseball player was selected the Big Ten's Most Valuable Player in 1984 and 1985 while a student at the University of Michigan?

A. Barry Larkin.

Q. What late-May festivity held in Alma features Scottish music and centuries-old athletic sporting events?

A. Highland Festival and Games.

Q. During Joseph P. Schmidt's thirteen-year stay with the Detroit Lions from 1953 to 1965, how many years was he the team captain?

A. Ten.

Q. What University of Michigan football coach created the "point-a-minute" teams at the turn of the century?

A. Fielding Yost.

Q. What are the colors of Northern Michigan University athletic teams?

A. Old gold and olive green.

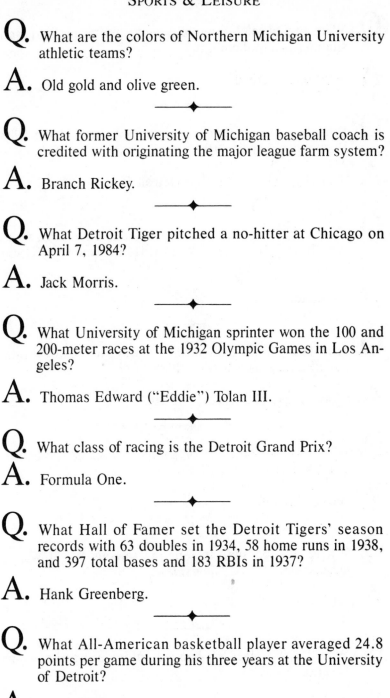

Q. What former University of Michigan baseball coach is credited with originating the major league farm system?

A. Branch Rickey.

Q. What Detroit Tiger pitched a no-hitter at Chicago on April 7, 1984?

A. Jack Morris.

Q. What University of Michigan sprinter won the 100 and 200-meter races at the 1932 Olympic Games in Los Angeles?

A. Thomas Edward ("Eddie") Tolan III.

Q. What class of racing is the Detroit Grand Prix?

A. Formula One.

Q. What Hall of Famer set the Detroit Tigers' season records with 63 doubles in 1934, 58 home runs in 1938, and 397 total bases and 183 RBIs in 1937?

A. Hank Greenberg.

Q. What All-American basketball player averaged 24.8 points per game during his three years at the University of Detroit?

A. David DeBuschere.

Q. What annual celebration of German heritage is held each summer in Frankenmuth?

A. Bavarian Festival.

Q. What was the final score of the last game of the 1988 Pistons vs. Lakers NBA championship playoffs?

A. Los Angeles Lakers 108, Detroit Pistons 105.

Q. Where is the nation's largest wooden shoe factory, in which visitors may watch craftsmen carve "Klompens"?

A. Holland.

Q. How many times did Detroit's Harry Heilmann win the American League batting title?

A. Four: 1921, 1923, 1925, and 1927.

Q. Who purchased the Detroit Lions for $225,000 on February 10, 1940?

A. Fred Wandell, Jr.

Q. Where is it possible to tour the famous World War II submarine, U.S.S. *Silversides?*

A. Muskegon.

Q. What Detroit Tiger left-handed outfielder was known as "Wahoo Sam"?

A. Samuel Earl Crawford.

Q. In 1940, what Detroit Red Wings player became the first member to win the Hart Trophy as the National Hockey League's Most Valuable Player?

A. Ebenezer ("Ebbie") R. Goodfellow.

Q. What state-of-the-art sports facility is replacing Jenison Field House at Michigan State University?

A. The Jack Breslin Student Events Center.

Q. Who has been the only Detroit Tiger to receive the *Sporting News* Rookie of the Year award?

A. Harvey Kuenn (1953).

Q. What University of Michigan All-American halfback in 1939 and 1940 became known for his "old 98" jersey?

A. Thomas ("Tom") Dudley Harmon.

Q. For how many years did Charles E. Forsythe serve as Michigan high school state director of athletics?

A. Thirty-six.

Q. An Olympic training center is headquartered at what Michigan university?

A. Northern Michigan University.

Q. What four Detroit Tigers have stolen second base, third base, and home?

A. Bill Donovan, Bill Couchlin, Ty Cobb, and Jackie Tavener.

Q. At what university did John J. MacInnes become the winningest hockey coach in college history?

A. Michigan Technological University (from 1956 to 1982).

Q. What University of Michigan football coach is credited with the two-platoon system?

A. Herbert Orin ("Fritz") Crisler.

Q. How many consecutive games did Hudson High School win from 1968 to 1975?

A. Seventy-two (a national record).

Q. Where was major leaguer Kirk Gibson born?

A. Pontiac.

Q. What lightweight world professional boxing champion from 1896 to 1899 was known as the "Saginaw Kid"?

A. George Henry Lavigne.

Q. How many batting titles did Ty Cobb win during his professional career?

A. Twelve.

Q. What historic event took place at Tiger Stadium on July 13, 1934?

A. Babe Ruth's 700th career home run.

Q. In what years was Sparky Anderson named American League Manager of the Year?

A. 1984 and 1987.

———◆———

Q. What quarterback who played with the Detroit Lions from 1950 to 1957 led the team to three world championships?

A. Robert ("Bobby") Layne.

———◆———

Q. What summer event in Grand Haven features tours of Great Lakes ships and band entertainment?

A. Coast Guard Festival.

———◆———

Q. Where is the international balloon championships held?

A. Battle Creek (in July).

———◆———

Q. What University of Michigan pitcher and first baseman won two American League batting titles in 1920 and 1922?

A. George Sisler.

———◆———

Q. How many seasons did Alexander Peter Delvecchio serve as team captain of the Detroit Red Wings?

A. Twelve.

———◆———

Q. What Eastern Michigan University track star was called the "One-Man-Gang"?

A. Hayes W. Jones.

Q. How many letters did Benjamin ("Bennie") Oosterbaan earn while at the University of Michigan?

A. Nine.

———◆———

Q. What four Detroit Tigers have won American League batting titles since World War II?

A. George Kell (1949), Al Kaline (1955), Harvey Kuenn (1959), and Norm Cash (1961).

———◆———

Q. Eastern Michigan University is a member of what athletic conference?

A. Mid-American Conference.

———◆———

Q. How many times did Marion Van Oosten Ladewig win the world's championship in bowling?

A. Five.

———◆———

Q. During the 1984–85 basketball season, Northern Michigan University set a school record with how many consecutive wins?

A. Thirteen.

———◆———

Q. Pitching for the Detroit Tigers from 1941 to 1952 and again in 1956, Virgil Oliver Trucks earned what nickname?

A. "Firetrucks."

———◆———

Q. Who was the University of Detroit's winningest basketball coach?

A. Robert James ("Call") Calihan.

Q. What was the actual name of Michigan middleweight boxing champion Stanley Ketchel?

A. Stanislau Kiecal.

---◆---

Q. Hayes Wendell Jones won a gold medal in what event during the 1964 Olympics in Tokyo?

A. 110 meter hurdles.

---◆---

Q. What Michigan community is host of the Alpenfest?

A. Gaylord.

---◆---

Q. Who owned the Detroit Red Wings from 1933 to 1952?

A. James Norris.

---◆---

Q. What Michigan State University head coach was named Football Coach of the Year in 1952?

A. Clarence L. ("Biggie") Munn.

---◆---

Q. What Holland attraction contains a 1920 Locomobile in its collection, in addition to a large display of other types of vehicles?

A. Poll Museum of Transportation.

---◆---

Q. What two Detroit Tigers hold the team record for fewest strikeouts during a single season with thirteen each?

A. Charlie Gehringer (1936) and Harvey Kuenn (1954).

Q. What is the nation's largest air-supported domed stadium?

A. The Silverdome (in Pontiac).

———◆———

Q. Who served as baseball coach at the University of Michigan from 1921 to 1958?

A. Raymond Lyle Fisher.

———◆———

Q. How many times was Gordon ("Gordie") Howe voted Most Valuable Player in the National Hockey League?

A. Six (and once in the World Hockey Association).

———◆———

Q. What Detroit Tiger won All-State honors for Detroit Catholic Central in baseball and basketball?

A. Frank Tanana.

———◆———

Q. What special event is held at South Haven in late July?

A. Blueberry Festival.

———◆———

Q. What Southpaw native of Zeeland spent twenty-five years in the major leagues?

A. Jim Kaat.

———◆———

Q. What is the nation's largest indoor–outdoor museum complex?

A. Henry Ford Museum and Greenfield Village (Dearborn).

Q. What team that was purchased on June 30, 1934, for less than $8,000 was moved to Detroit and renamed the Lions?

A. The Portsmouth Spartans.

Q. In 1969 Tiger fans selected what player as their favorite all-time third baseman?

A. George Kell.

Q. What Flint coach in 1963 became the first high-school coach to be inducted into the Michigan Sports Hall of Fame?

A. Guy V. Houston.

Q. During what years did Michael Herbert ("Dad") Butler serve the University of Detroit as track coach and trainer?

A. 1927 to 1944.

Q. Northern Michigan University sports teams are known by what nickname?

A. Wildcats.

Q. What University of Michigan football player earned All-American collegiate honors in 1925, 1926, and 1927?

A. Benjamin ("Bennie") Oosterbaan.

Q. Who did Ray ("Sugar Ray") Robinson defeat in 1951 to win his first middleweight title?

A. Jake LaMotta.

Q. Where was the first professional hockey team organized in 1903?

A. Houghton.

———◆———

Q. What national tennis event did Dr. Allen Stowe first bring to Kalamazoo College in 1943?

A. National Junior and Boys Championships.

———◆———

Q. What Detroit native was named the American League's Most Valuable Player in 1944 and 1945?

A. Harold Newhouser.

———◆———

Q. Who in 1923 became Michigan State's first coach of all sports?

A. Ralph H. Young.

———◆———

Q. What was the length of George ("The Gipper") Gipp's famous dropkick field goal that put him into the record books at Notre Dame?

A. Sixty-two yards.

———◆———

Q. Who was the University of Detroit's first All-American?

A. Lloyd F. Brazil.

———◆———

Q. Ron Kramer attended what high school, where he received All-State honors in track and football during the early 1950s?

A. East Detroit High School.

Q. In what year did the Detroit Tigers win their first World Series?

A. 1935 (vs. Chicago).

Q. Who was Michigan State University's first and only athlete to win ten letters?

A. Layman L. ("Frim") Frimodig.

Q. What graduate of Wyandotte Roosevelt High School won a record eleven national archery titles?

A. Ann P. Marston.

Q. What pitcher, who joined the Detroit Tigers in 1913, went on to become one of baseball's most successful scouts?

A. Aloysius ("Wish") Egan.

Q. What Michigan weight lifter set twenty-six world records between 1948 and 1964?

A. Norbert Schemansky.

Q. Who is considered to be the all-time greatest Michigan State football player?

A. George Webster.

Q. What long-time Detroit Northwestern High School football coach and athletic director was named Michigan High School Coach of the Year in 1959?

A. Sam Isaac Bishop.

Q. Michigan native Sheila Young won gold, silver, and bronze medals in what event in the 1976 Olympics?

A. Speed skating.

———◆———

Q. In what year did the Detroit Tigers set the American League record for the highest single season batting average?

A. 1921 (.316).

———◆———

Q. Gordon ("Gordie") Howe set an all-time National League scoring record with how many points?

A. 1,850 (801 goals, 1049 assists).

———◆———

Q. In 1925 what University of Michigan quarterback led the Big Ten in scoring?

A. Benjamin Friedman (52 points).

———◆———

Q. Who was voted Tiger of the Year in 1984?

A. Willie Hernandez.

———◆———

Q. Who was considered Michigan's most successful tennis coach of teen-age players, leading her Hamtramck teams to sixteen Michigan titles from 1949 to 1965?

A. Jean R. Hoxie.

———◆———

Q. What canoeist is memorialized fourteen miles west of Oscoda on Au Sable River?

A. Jerry Curley.

Q. In what baseball scandal was Detroit native Eddie Cicotte involved?

A. The Black Sox scandal of 1919.

Q. What is the seating capacity of the Silverdome?

A. 80,638.

Q. What Wolverine cycling coach produced three world champions?

A. Mike Walden.

Q. In what Michigan community was Michigan State University's star athlete and long-time assistant athletic director Lyman L. ("Frim") Frimodig born?

A. Calumet.

Q. During what mid-May celebration does Holland salute its Dutch heritage?

A. Tulip Time Festival.

Q. What Detroit Tiger homered in his first time at bat in the major leagues at Tiger Stadium?

A. Reggie Sanders (September 1, 1974).

Q. What Fremont firm takes visitors on a minitrain guided tour of their facilities, showing the step-by-step processing and packaging of baby food?

A. Gerber Products Company.

Q. What Wayne State University track star won a gold medal as a member of the U.S. 440-meter relay team at the 1948 Olympics in London?

A. Lorenzo C. Wright.

———◆———

Q. In what two years did Michigan State University head football coach Hugh Duffy Daugherty win national Coach of the Year honors?

A. 1956 and 1965.

———◆———

Q. What pioneer Michigan basketball player headed the Detroit Athletic Club for twenty years and founded the Cadillac Athletic Club in 1927?

A. Jacob Mazer.

———◆———

Q. Speedboat racing's winningest driver, William Edward Muncey, was born in what Michigan community?

A. Ferndale.

———◆———

Q. What Bay City event in early July is rated as one of the most exciting celebrations of its type in the nation?

A. Fireworks Festival.

———◆———

Q. How many freshman track records did Robert ("Bob") Poorman Ufer break at the University of Michigan in 1939?

A. Nine.

———◆———

Q. What Michigan golfer became a member of the prestigious Masters Rules Committee in 1955?

A. Warren W. Orlick.

Q. What trophy is collected by the winner of the annual Michigan State–Indiana football game?

A. The Old Brass Spittoon.

Q. What Detroit coach and priest staged football games between Catholic Central and Boys Town in 1944 and 1945 at Briggs Stadium?

A. Father James E. Martin.

Q. During his career as coach at Flint Northern High School, Guy V. Houston's teams won how many Saginaw Valley Conference Championships?

A. Twelve.

Q. Harold Newhouser, left-handed Detroit Tigers pitcher of the 1940s and early 1950s, was known by what nickname?

A. "Prince Hal."

Q. What attraction at Whitefish Point, Upper Peninsula, features a display of six ships sunk nearby?

A. Great Lakes Shipwreck Museum.

Q. Jay Vincent of Michigan State began his professional career with what NBA franchise?

A. Dallas Mavericks.

Q. What Detroit Lions player from 1948 to 1954 is considered by many the most famous middle-guard in the history of pro football?

A. Lester ("Bing") Bingaman.

Q. What member of the University of Michigan football team was voted Most Valuable Player by his teammates in 1934?

A. Gerald Rudolph Ford.

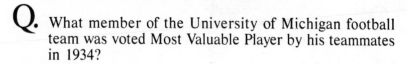

Q. Who managed the Detroit Tigers from 1907 to 1920?

A. Hugh A. Jennings.

Q. What Brazilian won the Detroit Grand Prix in 1986, 1987, and 1988?

A. Ayrton Senna.

Q. What Detroit-born major league pitcher has allowed the most career grand slams?

A. Milt Pappas (nine).

Q. What Michigan State placekicker set a Big Ten Conference record for longest field goal of sixty-three yards in 1981?

A. Morten Anderson.

Q. How many gold medals did Michigan athlete Greg Barton win at the 1988 Summer Olympics in Seoul, Korea?

A. Two.

Q. What Michigan golfer won the International Seniors Championships at Gleneagles, Scotland, in 1973?

A. Charles ("Chuck") Kocsis.

Q. What University of Michigan athlete set a NCAA high jump record in 1940 at six feet, seven and three-quarters inches?

A. Donald B. Canham.

------◆------

Q. At what Sault Sainte Marie attraction does a 550-foot operational freighter contain the world's largest Great Lakes maritime museum?

A. Museum Ship Valley Camp.

------◆------

Q. What Detroit native has pitched for the most big league teams?

A. Dick Littlefield (ten clubs in nine seasons).

------◆------

Q. In what year did John H. Kobs coach the Michigan State University baseball team to a Big Ten Championship?

A. 1954.

------◆------

Q. What Michigan golfer won twenty-two consecutive matches in Michigan amateur championships during his career?

A. Glenn H. Johnson.

------◆------

Q. The *Sporting News* American League Rookie Pitcher of the Year award went to what Detroit Tiger in 1987?

A. Mike Henneman.

------◆------

Q. What 1941 All-American center at the University of Detroit went on to play with the Chicago Cardinals and the Detroit Lions?

A. Vincent J. Banonis.

Q. What Detroit Tiger was voted Most Valuable Player of the 1968 Detroit vs. Saint Louis World Series?

A. Mickey Lolich.

———◆———

Q. What Michigan race car driver won the Indianapolis 500 in 1941, 1947, and 1948?

A. Mauri Rose.

———◆———

Q. Who received the title of Detroit's "Grand Old Man of Sports"?

A. Michael Herbert ("Dad") Butler.

———◆———

Q. Of the fifteen head coaches employed by the Detroit Tigers during their first forty-six years, which held the position for the most years?

A. George W. Wilson (eight years).

———◆———

Q. Having played on four national title teams, who is Michigan's highest rated polo player?

A. Jack Ivory.

———◆———

Q. Who was the last Detroit Tiger to lead the American League in home runs?

A. Hank Greenberg (44 in 1946).

———◆———

Q. What was the last world speedboat record set by Garfield A. Wood in 1932?

A. 124.91 m.p.h.

Q. By what nickname was Detroit's Joe Louis (Barrow) known?

A. "The Brown Bomber."

Q. Where was Michigan Olympic speed-skater Richard McDermott born?

A. Essexville.

Q. What Detroit Tiger was the last American Leaguer to lead in wins, strikeouts, and earned runs average in one year?

A. Hal Newhauser (1945: 25 wins, 212 strikeouts, and 1.81 ERA).

Q. Charles ("Chuck") Davey, Michigan's boxing commissioner from 1965 to 1980, set a NCAA record during the late 1940s with how many boxing championship titles?

A. Four.

Q. In whose honor is the Kalamazoo tennis stadium named?

A. Dr. Allen B. Stone.

Q. Who managed the Detroit Tigers to back-to-back pennants in 1934 and 1935?

A. Mickey Cochrane.

Q. What Michigan State football player placed fourth in the Heisman Trophy balloting in 1985?

A. Lorenzo White.

Q. What Michigan table tennis figure is credited with establishing "ping-pong diplomacy" between the Peoples Republic of China and the United States in 1971?

A. Graham B. Steenhoven.

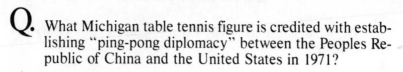

Q. Who was the last Detroit Tiger to lead the American League in stolen bases?

A. Marty McManus (23 in 1930).

Q. Who was the first two-time Masters Tournament Champion who later served for many years as the head pro at the Detroit Golf Club?

A. Horton Smith.

Q. Who holds the Detroit Tiger club record for career wins?

A. George ("Hooks") Dauss (221 over 15 years).

Q. Who on October 1, 1901, defeated race car driver Alexander Winton in a ten-mile race at Grosse Pointe to become U.S. track champion?

A. Henry Ford.

Q. Who became sole owner of the Detroit Tigers in 1935?

A. Walter O. Briggs, Sr.

Q. In what event at the 1964 Winter Olympics in Innsbruck did speed-skater Richard McDermott set a world's record in winning a gold medal?

A. Men's 500 meter.

SCIENCE & NATURE

C H A P T E R S I X

Q. Because of its mineral resources, what area of Michigan has been called the state's "treasure chest?"

A. Keweenaw Peninsula.

Q. What is the only species of bear native to Michigan?

A. Black bear.

Q. Presently what is the most planted peach variety in Michigan?

A. Redhaven.

Q. The Grand Rapids planetarium is named in honor of what astronaut?

A. Roger B. Chaffee.

Q. At 45 feet deep and 200 feet across, what is Michigan's largest spring?

A. Kitch-iti-kipi Spring, Palms Book State Park.

Q. During its peak production year of 1882, how many board feet of lumber were processed at Saginaw?

A. 1,011,000,000.

———◆———

Q. The wolverine is a member of what animal family?

A. Weasel.

———◆———

Q. Approximately how many acres of Michigan farmland is utilized for growing asparagus?

A. Twenty thousand.

———◆———

Q. Who was Michigan's first geologist?

A. Douglass Houghton.

———◆———

Q. The area around Escanaba became famous for what type of decorative wood?

A. Bird's-eye maple.

———◆———

Q. What oil and gas fields were discovered south of Clare in 1930?

A. Vernon fields.

———◆———

Q. Approximately 140 kinds of hybrid lilacs are featured at what Ann Arbor garden attraction?

A. Nichols Arboretum.

Q. What variety accounts for almost 90 percent of Michigan's grape production?

A. Concord.

Q. The first moving pictures of what celestial body were produced in Pontiac on June 19, 1934?

A. The Sun.

Q. What two Jackson natives have been to the moon and back?

A. Colonel James McDivitt and Major Alfred Worden.

Q. Isle Royale covers approximately how many square miles?

A. 210.

Q. Where were peregrine falcons reintroduced to Michigan in 1986 after a twenty-year absence?

A. Downtown Grand Rapids.

Q. Beaver Island has how many natural lakes?

A. Seven.

Q. Where does Michigan rank nationally in the production of iron ore?

A. Second only to Minnesota.

Q. In the early history of Cascade, the local mineral springs were promoted as curing what affliction?

A. Saint Vitus's dance (chorea).

Q. Over the past fifty years, by what percentage has the bluebird population of Michigan declined?

A. Ninety percent.

Q. What is Michigan's smallest state park?

A. Wagner Falls.

Q. Traverse City proudly carries what title?

A. Cherry Capital of the World.

Q. What tree was most valued by the early Indians of Michigan as a source of building materials for houses and canoes?

A. Birch.

Q. By what term are fresh, unfrozen smelt identified in the fishing industry?

A. "Green" fish.

Q. Where on August 19, 1929, was the nation's first all-metal dirigible successfully flown?

A. Grosse Ile Airport.

Q. In the production of what fungi does Michigan rank third in the nation?

A. Mushrooms.

Q. What Detroit River island was known as Swan or Rattlesnake Island to the Indians and later called Hog Island (Isle au Cochon) by French settlers?

A. Belle Isle.

Q. In the peak year of 1907, how many tons of bituminous coal were mined from beneath southeastern Michigan?

A. 2,035,858.

Q. Who perfected the electrolytic cell to enable the practical extraction of such elements as bromine, chlorine, and lithium?

A. Dr. Herbert H. Dow.

Q. What type of geological formation is the Mason Hogback, which extends from north of Lansing to near Leslie?

A. Esker (a ridge of glacial gravel).

Q. What is a grove of sugar maple trees called?

A. A sugar bush.

Q. How high above sea level are the surfaces of both Lake Michigan and Lake Huron?

A. 579 feet.

Q. Where was Michigan's first Bessemer steel converter erected in 1864?

A. Wyandotte.

———◆———

Q. What is the greatest depth of Lake Michigan?

A. 923 feet.

———◆———

Q. In what year did the University of Michigan become the first college in the nation to offer courses in bacteriology?

A. 1889.

———◆———

Q. On January 25, 1945, Grand Rapids became the first city to introduce what additive to its municipal water supply?

A. Fluoride.

———◆———

Q. Among the Chippewa Indians what was the most important religious and magic society?

A. The Mide.

———◆———

Q. What Upper Peninsula attraction offers a tour through 2,600 feet of underground drifts and tunnels to view iron mining?

A. Iron Mountain Iron Mine.

———◆———

Q. Corrective surgery on what part of a human heart was first performed in Detroit on July 3, 1952?

A. Mitral valve.

Q. Michigan leads the nation in the production of what legumes?

A. Dry edible beans.

———◆———

Q. Sylvania Recreation Area in the Upper Peninsula is a part of what national forest?

A. Ottawa National Forest.

———◆———

Q. What wonder of the mining world is on permanent display at Quincy Nine, near Hancock, in Upper Michigan?

A. Norberg Hoist (the world's largest steam-powered mine hoist).

———◆———

Q. In 1829 what item did William A. Burt invent while living in Washington?

A. Typographer (the nation's first writing machine).

———◆———

Q. Lake Michigan covers how many square miles?

A. 22,300.

———◆———

Q. Mohawkite, a mineral compound named for the community and mine where it was produced in the early 1900s, contains what two substances?

A. Copper and arsenic.

———◆———

Q. In 1966 Michigan became the first state in the nation to adopt what type of dairy inspection regulations?

A. Grade A fluid milk laws.

Q. What instrument was invented by Dr. John Harvey Kellogg in the late 1800s to measure muscle strength?

A. The universal dynamometer.

Q. Kalamazoo and nearby areas are considered the birthplace of what vegetable industry?

A. Celery.

Q. Where is the Coppertown U.S.A. Mining Museum?

A. Calumet.

Q. At the University of Michigan on June 22, 1896, Mary Stone became the first Chinese woman in the United States to receive what degree?

A. Doctor of Medicine.

Q. How many types of native fish exist in Michigan waters?

A. 149.

Q. What nuclear research tool recently brought international fame to Michigan State University?

A. The National Superconducting Cyclotron Laboratory.

Q. Legislators in 1965 selected what fish as the official state fish?

A. Trout.

Q. What state park northeast of Grayling features the Lumberman's Museum?

A. Hartwick Pines State Park.

Q. What is the largest lake in the Upper Peninsula?

A. Lake Gogebic.

Q. Michigan annually produces ten million pounds of what member of the cabbage family?

A. Cauliflower.

Q. What Ishpeming native received the Nobel Prize for chemistry?

A. Dr. Glenn Seaborg.

Q. With Michigan ranked seventh in the nation in honey production, how many pounds of beeswax are produced in the state annually?

A. Almost 75,000.

Q. What is the official Michigan state bird?

A. Robin.

Q. In 1894 Parke-Davis became the first firm in the nation to market an antitoxin for what malady?

A. Diphtheria.

Q. Approximately how many single-dip ice cream cones could be filled with Michigan's annual ice cream production?

A. 805,000,000.

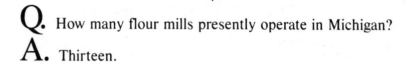

Q. How many flour mills presently operate in Michigan?

A. Thirteen.

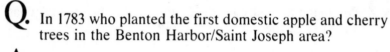

Q. In 1783 who planted the first domestic apple and cherry trees in the Benton Harbor/Saint Joseph area?

A. William Burnett.

Q. What affectionate nickname was given to Henry Ford's famous 1908 Model T?

A. "Tin Lizzie."

Q. For what metal is the Keweenaw Peninsula most famous?

A. Copper.

Q. Where does Michigan rank in relationship to the other states in the production of apples?

A. Second.

Q. What type of cranial surgery was practiced by some early Michigan Indian tribes?

A. Trephining (removing a circular disk of bone from the skull).

Q. What fresh-market vegetable produced in Michigan is the third highest in sales volume?

A. Carrots.

———◆———

Q. The Pierce Stocking Scenic Drive offers spectacular views of what National Lakeshore near Empire?

A. Sleeping Bear Dunes.

———◆———

Q. What percentage of the nation's red tart cherries are grown in Michigan?

A. Nearly 80 percent.

———◆———

Q. During the 1880s and 90s, what was the largest gold mine in Michigan?

A. Ropes (near Ishpeming).

———◆———

Q. In 1834 Kalamazoo County resident Hiram Moore received the nation's first patent for what type of farm equipment?

A. Combination harvester and thresher.

———◆———

Q. What national park is in Michigan?
A. Isle Royale.

———◆———

Q. The Kingman Museum of Natural History is in what Michigan arboretum?

A. Leila Arboretum (at Battlecreek).

Q. What three animals appear on the Great Seal of Michigan?

A. Elk, moose, and eagle.

Q. When does the three-month commercial green bean harvest start in Michigan?

A. Early July.

Q. When production first started in 1871, what was the percentage of purity of the iron ore mined in the Republic area?

A. Eighty-eight percent.

Q. What road has been voted the most scenic in the state?

A. Brockway Mountain Drive near Copper Harbor.

Q. How long is Beaver Island?

A. Thirteen miles.

Q. What animal did early Michigan fur trappers call a skunk-bear?

A. Wolverine.

Q. For what purpose is approximately 90 percent of Michigan's corn crop used?

A. Livestock feed.

Q. Where does Michigan rank nationally in the production of blueberries?

A. First.

———◆———

Q. What food product line is produced at the Chelsea Milling Company in Chelsea?

A. Jiffy brand mixes.

———◆———

Q. Where in 1862 was the first laboratory established in the United States for steel analysis?

A. Wyandotte.

———◆———

Q. The Upper Tahquamenon Falls has been given what other name?

A. The Little Niagara.

———◆———

Q. Measuring over a hundred feet in width, the largest lock in America has what name?

A. Poe (Soo Canals).

———◆———

Q. In what month does Michigan's commercial grape harvest begin?

A. August (peaking in September).

———◆———

Q. Approximately how many species of trees grow in Michigan's 18.4 million acres of forest?

A. Sixty-five.

Q. What is the largest inland lake in Michigan?

A. Houghton Lake (covering thirty square miles in the north-central Lower Peninsula).

———◆———

Q. The Gogebic Iron Range became best known for what type of iron ore?

A. Soft red hematite.

———◆———

Q. In what year was the first great smelt run at Beulah on Crystal Lake?

A. 1922.

———◆———

Q. Michigan dairy regulations require what percentage of milkfat to be present in butter?

A. At least 80 percent.

———◆———

Q. What is the largest national forest in Michigan?

A. Ottawa National Forest.

———◆———

Q. How many pounds of cabbage are harvested annually in Michigan?

A. More than 46,000,000.

———◆———

Q. What were the two major food grains of the Algonquin Indians when the first Europeans arrived in Michigan?

A. Corn and wild rice.

Q. Italian, Blufre, and Stanley are the most popular varieties of what type of fruit grown commercially in Michigan?

A. Purple plums.

———◆———

Q. How long is Lake Michigan?

A. 307 miles.

———◆———

Q. Between the years of 1847 and 1883, what portion of the nation's total copper production came from Michigan?

A. One-half.

———◆———

Q. What unique bridge built in the Upper Peninsula in 1919 is supported by the water that is atmospherically forced under it?

A. Siphon Bridge, Manistique.

———◆———

Q. What type of tree provided the early Indians of Michigan with a source of sweetener?

A. Sugar maple.

———◆———

Q. What is the average production per acre of field corn in Michigan?

A. 105 bushels.

———◆———

Q. What facility at Cadillac provides an opportunity for viewing wildlife in natural surroundings?

A. Johnny's Wild Game and Fish Park.

Q. In September of 1986 what weather reporting station set a new state record for most precipitation in a single month at 19.26 inches?

A. Edmore.

Q. What is the most popular Michigan potato?

A. Russet Burbank.

Q. In 1900 what hormone was discovered by the Parke-Davis pharmaceutical firm in Detroit?

A. Adrenalin.

Q. What all-metal plane produced by Henry Ford in 1926 became the nation's first successful transport?

A. Ford Trimotor.

Q. Michigan leads the nation in the production of what mint extract?

A. Spearmint oil.

Q. What is the average size of a Michigan farm?

A. 181 acres.

Q. What name is applied to the scenic shore drive between Harbor Springs and Cross Village?

A. "Tunnel of Trees."

Q. What Michigan university is the only school in the nation with three medical schools on its campus?

A. Michigan State University.

———◆———

Q. The Van Buren County seat derives its name from what type of tree.

A. Paw Paw.

———◆———

Q. What animal heroine from the motion picture *Sequoia* was displayed during the 1930s and 40s near Bridgman?

A. Lady (the mountain lion).

———◆———

Q. Arnold F. Willat, born in Detroit in 1886, revolutionized the cosmetology industry by developing what process?

A. The cold permanent wave.

———◆———

Q. Michigan contains what two land regions?

A. The Superior Upland and the Great Lakes Plains.

———◆———

Q. Approximately how much of Michigan is covered by forests?

A. 19 million acres (over half of the state).

———◆———

Q. Meandering a distance of 260 miles, what is the longest river in Michigan?

A. The Grand River.

Q. In 1939 the Packard Motor Car Company became the first firm in the nation to introduce what automobile comfort feature?

A. Air conditioning.

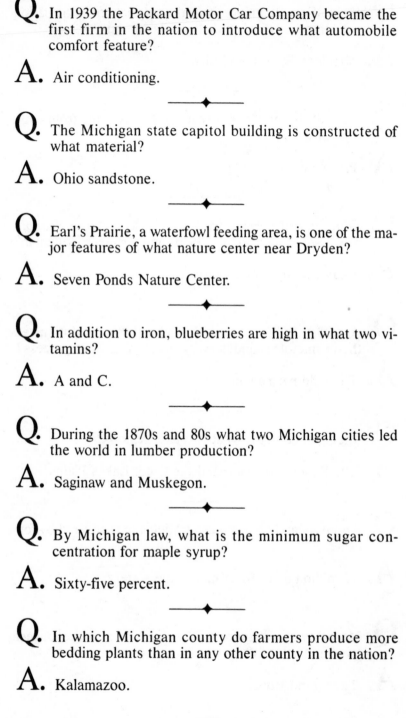

Q. The Michigan state capitol building is constructed of what material?

A. Ohio sandstone.

Q. Earl's Prairie, a waterfowl feeding area, is one of the major features of what nature center near Dryden?

A. Seven Ponds Nature Center.

Q. In addition to iron, blueberries are high in what two vitamins?

A. A and C.

Q. During the 1870s and 80s what two Michigan cities led the world in lumber production?

A. Saginaw and Muskegon.

Q. By Michigan law, what is the minimum sugar concentration for maple syrup?

A. Sixty-five percent.

Q. In which Michigan county do farmers produce more bedding plants than in any other county in the nation?

A. Kalamazoo.

Q. What is the largest staging area in the eastern United States for the sandhill crane?

A. Haehnle Sanctuary (near Grass Lake).

———◆———

Q. On April 28, 1897, Michigan selected what official state flower?

A. Apple Blossom.

———◆———

Q. What is the average length of smelt?

A. Eight to ten inches.

———◆———

Q. Blueberries require what type of soil for proper production?

A. Acidic.

———◆———

Q. What process was used by the Algonquin Indians to kill trees in the Michigan forests to create clearings in which to plant their crops?

A. Girdling.

———◆———

Q. Michigan is divided into how many soil conservation districts?

A. Eighty-three.

———◆———

Q. What is Michigan's largest volume fresh market vegetable crop?

A. Onions.

Q. Opened in 1904, what is the oldest freshwater aquarium in the nation?

A. Belle Isle Aquarium.

———◆———

Q. What is the largest lake on Isle Royale?

A. Siskiwit.

———◆———

Q. What Adrian resident patented the first practical seeding machine on August 25, 1840?

A. Joseph Gibbons.

———◆———

Q. Trout account for what percentage of Michigan's commercial fishing industry?

A. Four percent.

———◆———

Q. What large Michigan copper mass revered by local Indians is now on display at the Smithsonian Institution in Washington, D.C.?

A. The Ontonagon Boulder.

———◆———

Q. In 1912 what type of large mammals crossed the ice from Canada and established themselves on Isle Royale?

A. Moose.

———◆———

Q. Michigan ranks fourth in the nation in the production of what type of beans?

A. Snap green beans.

Q. Standard, Ranch Wild, Demi-Buff, Pastel, Violet, Pearl White, and Mahogany are all popular color classes of what Michigan product?

A. Mink pelts.

———◆———

Q. What is the largest island in Michigan waters?

A. Isle Royale.

———◆———

Q. The Keweenaw Peninsula witnessed the closing of its last copper mine in what year?

A. 1968.

———◆———

Q. What are the two major types of melons grown in Michigan?

A. Cantaloupe and watermelon.

———◆———

Q. Chicago capitalist Charles Mears, called the "Christopher Columbus of the West Coast," is honored by a state park near what Lake Michigan community?

A. Pentwater.

———◆———

Q. What revolutionary dental tool was patented by G. F. Green of Kalamazoo in 1875?

A. The electric dental drill.

———◆———

Q. Michigan's present commercial forest base has approximately how many acres?

A. 17.5 million.

Q. Weighing approximately 420 tons, in what mine near Rockland was Michigan's largest single mass of copper discovered?

A. The Old Michigan Mine.

Q. How many gallons of sap does it take to produce one gallon of maple syrup?

A. Forty.

Q. What is the highest-above-sea-level scenic drive in the Midwest?

A. Brockway Mountain Summit Drive.

Q. What county leads Michigan in sheep production?

A. Washtenaw.

Q. Where on September 1, 1914, was the Michigan record for most precipitation in a twenty-four-hour period set?

A. Bloomingdale (9.78 inches of rain).

Q. Although the area is not as well known for its agricultural activities as other areas of the state, how many farms are in the Upper Peninsula?

A. Over 2,250.

Q. What dairy product consumed by dieters is produced in Michigan at an annual rate of thirty to thirty-five thousand pounds?

A. Creamed cottage cheese.

Q. What is the major type of hay produced in Michigan?

A. Alfalfa.

Q. One pound of spearmint oil can flavor how many sticks of chewing gum?

A. 135,000.

Q. What Upper Peninsula county declares itself to be the "U.P. Dairy Capital"?

A. Menominee.

Q. How many pounds of refined copper were produced during 1916 and 1917 in the Keeweenaw Peninsula?

A. Almost 270,000,000.

Q. What altitude did Dr. Jean Piccard and his wife Jeannette reach in the Dow stratosphere balloon launched from Ford Airport in Dearborn on October 23, 1934?

A. Ten miles.

Q. The mining of what kind of rich iron ore was begun at Vulcan in 1874?

A. Blue hematite.

Q. What two means of storage did the early Indians of Michigan utilize for their grain crops?

A. Cribs and caches (pits).

Q. Michigan adopted what stone found in the northern tourist area as the official state stone?

A. Petoskey stone (fossil coral).

———◆———

Q. What famous pioneer wildlife photographer conducted many of his night photography experiments on Grand Island?

A. George Shiras III.

———◆———

Q. What was the weight of a single lump of pure copper discovered on Copper Falls Creek in 1845?

A. Approximately seven tons (14,000 pounds).

———◆———

Q. What Fort Mackinac surgeon between 1822 and 1830 discovered the gastronomic action of pepsin while conducting experiments on a gunshot patient?

A. Dr. William Beaumont.

———◆———

Q. What Michigan county leads the state in the production of fruit?

A. Berrien.

———◆———

Q. What tree was adopted as the official state tree on March 4, 1955?

A. White pine.

———◆———

Q. In 1985 approximately how many pounds of dry beans were harvested in Michigan?

A. 541,200,000.

Q. In 1965 nesting pairs of ospreys in Michigan dropped to what record low?

A. Fifty-one.

Q. The Star Theatre, with its ultraviolet and fluorescent murals, is part of what Flint astronomical facility?

A. Longway Planetarium.

Q. What Iron Mountain museum displays a dog-powered washer, a round metal icebox, and a man-eating clam shell?

A. The House of Yesteryear.

Q. How many types of weasels exist in Michigan?

A. Three.

Q. What attraction located just north of Holland features the blooms of over two million tulips each spring?

A. Veldheer Tulip Gardens.

Q. A few Michigan counties serve as summer homes for what rare yellow-breasted songbird?

A. Kirtland's warbler.

Q. What two national lakeshores are in Michigan?

A. Sleeping Bear Dunes and Pictured Rocks.

Q. What is the estimated number of cords of wood used as a fuel in Michigan each year?

A. 3.1 million.

———◆———

Q. Now ranking third in production in the nation, veal production was first recognized as an industry in Michigan in what year?

A. 1972.

———◆———

Q. What is the length of Isle Royale?

A. Forty-four miles.

———◆———

Q. What is the second largest zoo in Michigan?

A. John Ball Zoological Gardens (in Grand Rapids).

———◆———

Q. What variety of onion accounts for the greatest percentage of Michigan's crop?

A. Yellow globe.

———◆———

Q. In the winter of 1985–86 what small fur-bearing mammal was reintroduced to the Pigeon River Country State Forest and the Manistee National Forest?

A. The pine marten.

———◆———

Q. The pneumatic hammer was patented by what Detroit resident on January 30, 1894?

A. C. B. King.

Q. Which of the almost 185,000 pear trees in Michigan is the most common variety?

A. Bartlett.

———◆———

Q. From 1870 to 1890 what was the average annual consumption rate of Michigan's forest by the lumber industry?

A. 33,000 acres per year.

———◆———

Q. Michigan was the first state in the nation to enact standards for what meat product?

A. Ground pork.

———◆———

Q. What is the amount of area covered by Lake Saint Clair?

A. 460 square miles.

———◆———

Q. In what section of the state are most of Michigan's sugar beets grown?

A. The Thumb.

———◆———

Q. Michigan ranks second in the nation in the production of what type of cherries?

A. Sweet.

———◆———

Q. How many varieties of annuals are on display at the Michigan State University Horticultural Gardens.

A. More than 800.

Q. What Michigan aeronautics pioneer discovered the lifting ability of the upper surface of a wing?

A. Augustus Moore Herring.

———◆———

Q. What is the primary function of the Seney National Wildlife Refuge?

A. Migratory refuge.

———◆———

Q. What is the maximum depth of Lake Huron?

A. 750 feet.

———◆———

Q. What two areas of Michigan are the most productive regions for growing dry beans?

A. The Bay-Thumb and Saginaw Valley.

———◆———

Q. Michigan has how many national forests?

A. Four: Ottawa, Hiawatha, Huron, and Manistee.

———◆———

Q. What variety of wheat widely used by the state's major cereal producers leads production in Michigan?

A. Eastern soft white winter wheat.

———◆———

Q. What small bird is listed as one of Michigan's most endangered species?

A. The piping plover.

Q. In 1887 W. A. Smith of Grand Rapids became the first salaried individual to hold what law enforcement position in the state?

A. Fish and game warden.

Q. Of the approximately 125 pairs of bald eagles now nesting in Michigan, two-thirds of them are found in what part of the state?

A. Upper Peninsula.

Q. With the help of modern technology, each Micnigan farmer is able to produce enough food to feed himself and how many additional people?

A. Seventy-eight.

Q. What is Michigan's leading poultry enterprise?

A. Egg production.

Q. Gaylord is home to what wilderness adventure display featuring sixty exhibits of mounted wildlife?

A. Call of the Wild Museum.

Q. What is the largest body of fresh water in the nation?

A. Lake Michigan.

Q. With an annual harvest of 13.5 million pounds, what is the most common type of pepper grown in Michigan?

A. Green (also called bell or globe).

Q. What Grand Rapids resident invented the first practical carpet sweeper in 1876?

A. M. R. Bissell.

---◆---

Q. What is the resident population of wolverines in the wilds of Michigan?

A. None.

---◆---

Q. The Abrams Planetarium is on the campus of what Michigan university?

A. Michigan State University.

---◆---

Q. What is the approximate length of Lake Huron?

A. 206 miles.

---◆---

Q. In what year were tomatoes first grown commercially in Michigan?

A. 1860.

---◆---

Q. What mammal is harvested by hunters in Michigan at an annual rate of 60,000 to 120,000, depending upon the hunting season and annual regulations?

A. White-tailed (or Virginia) deer.

---◆---

Q. Michigan leads the nation in the production of cucumbers for what purpose?

A. Pickling.

Q. What was the weight of the largest silver nugget ever found in the Phoenix area?

A. Eight and three-fourths pounds.

———◆———

Q. The Seney National Wildlife Refuge, noted for its large population of Canadian geese, encompasses how many acres?

A. 95,455.

———◆———

Q. What record number of now extinct passenger pigeons were killed on the migratory flyway at Shelby in a single year?

A. Over 700,000.

———◆———

Q. How many eggs are produced in Michigan each year?

A. Over 1.5 billion.

———◆———

Q. What Michigan crop has grown from a mere eight thousand acres in 1924 to a present annual planting in excess of one million acres?

A. Soybeans.

———◆———

Q. Found mainly in Michigan's Upper Peninsula, what gemstone was adopted as the state gem in 1972?

A. Chlorastrolite (also called Isle Royale green stone or greenstone).

———◆———

Q. What is the estimated number of bee colonies in Michigan?

A. 80,000 to 1,000,000.